HELP! I T.

"I liked the idea of how to find a physician, among the maze of so-called "professionals," who really knows what he is doing in terms of treating this disorder. This is needed more now than ever before. Of course your comments are not going to make you any friends among the managed care community. I certainly think it is time for people to recognize what professionals have known all along. Not all professionals are created equal and not all have the same skills or abilities or interests.

Your description of panic attacks and your treatment guide are very succinct and clear. They offer up-to-date material that gives people a very clear understanding of exactly why they might be experiencing the problem that they are having and how to get treatment for it."

— Lawrence S. Kuhn, M.D.
  Assistant Clinical Professor of Psychiatry,
  St. Louis University, St. Louis, MO
  Chairman, Dept. of Psychiatry,
  DePaul Health Center, St. Louis, MO

HELP!
I THINK
I'M DYING!

PANIC
ATTACKS
& PHOBIAS

by Abbot Lee Granoff, M.D.
Board Certified Psychiatrist

Eco Images • Virginia Beach, Virginia

Dedicated to my patients who make my life meaningful and to all those people and families who are suffering needlessly

TABLE OF CONTENTS

CHART AND DIAGRAMS

ACKNOWLEDGMENTS

Writing a book isn't easy. I don't consider myself an author, but I have seen so much unnecessary suffering that I knew this story had to be told.

I want to thank Jean Klein who made a valiant effort at collaborating with me on the first attempt at a more comprehensive edition of this book. I appreciate the time she spent listening to my ramblings and then putting them into an organized fashion. That organization was the basis of this book.

Thanks to the Upjohn Company for allowing me to use pictures from their booklet "The Biochemical Basis for Anxiety" which so vividly shows how the neuroanatomy, neurochemistry and neurophysiology of anxiety fit together and work. A picture is surely worth a thousand words. I also want to thank the Upjohn Company for allowing me to use their slides from "Panic Disorder Teaching Slide Set" and from "Panic and Agoraphobia" for the basis of my video explanation of panic attacks and agoraphobia.

Thanks to the American Psychiatric Association for allowing me to use portions of the *DSM-IV* to describe the anxiety disorders and to use their *Psychiatric Glossary* as the basis for my glossary.

A special thanks to my many patients who educated me about panic attacks and phobias. A double thanks to those patients (Sheryl S., Elayne G., Phillip S., Barbara G., Gene P., Alice P., Donna B., Wendy D. and Barbara M.) who encouraged me to write this book, who proofed the manuscripts and offered suggestions and criticism. Without your help the book would not flow as smoothly as it does. A triple thanks to those patients (Brian B., Sheryl S., Elayne G., Kevin M., Don T. and Barbara M.) who allowed me to videotape them telling their story, as only they could tell it.

A special appreciation and thanks to Laurie Szoke who helped me to obtain materials and information on panic disorder. She also helped me get local speaking engagements which allowed me to fine tune my talk on panic attacks and phobias. And she encouraged and supported me in my effort to produce this book.

A special thanks to Lesli Legum for guiding me in the right directions for the video tape production. I also appreciate her critique and suggestions to make it a better product.

A warm thanks and kudos to David and Trish Mimms of Video Atlantic. Their creativity, versatility and knowledge of the video industry rescued the initial video from the brink of death.

A very special thanks to my high school friend Mike Klein for creating my corporate name – MIND MATTERS.

My thanks and appreciation to my medical school professors: S. Rubin Bruesch, MD; Alex Fedinec, MD; H. Max West, MD and Gene Stollerman, MD all at the University of Tennessee in Memphis.

My humble and deep appreciation to the psychiatrists at Loyola University Stritch School of Medicine who provided me with the tools and skills to help heal others. Charles Hillenbrand, MD, my mentor, friend and greatest supporter deserves my life long gratitude for showing me that there is science to psychiatry and that diagnosis, treatment and results could be replicated. He guided me to Loyola where Jackson Smith, MD chaired a department that had no equal in teaching cutting-edge psychiatry. His faculty included: Jeff Levy, MD, my second mentor; in addition to Robert deVito, MD; Domina Renshaw, MD; Anthony D'Agostino, MD; Patrick Staunton, MD; Frank Roach, MD and Marvin DeHahn, MD. Dr. deVito, current department chairman, continues to run a superb program.

My switch to one of the three best biological psychiatric research centers in the country, Illinois State Psychiatric Institute, opened new realms of the field for me – biological research and psychoanalysis. I appreciate the broadening of my horizons by the staff: Lee Weiss, MD; Mertin Gill, MD; Jack Weinberg, MD and John Davis, MD. They all helped round out whatever rough edges were left.

My hats off to Loyola and Illinois State Psychiatric Institute. These institutions and their faculties receive too little recognition for the great contributions they have made and continue to make to one of the toughest specialties in medicine – Psychiatry.

Thanks to my friends Larry and Brenda Klar for proofing the manuscripts and offering constructive criticism and to John Crow of Memory Bank Computers for his computer expertise. Thanks also to Vickie and Paul Shufer from Eco Images for revisions, computer help and guiding me through the complex process of publishing. This book would not exist if they hadn't come along and given so much of themselves.

Appreciation and thanks to Dr. David Sheehan for his support, help, encouragement and suggestions for this book. His very successful book *The Anxiety Disease* is the only other book I recommend to my patients on this subject.

Deepest appreciation and thanks to my wife Ann, my life's companion, who put up with me during the months of planning, writing and editing. I will miss the evenings and weekends arguing about having to read yet another revised manuscript. Without her help the grammar, punctuation, flow and content would still be a nightmare. Without her undying support and encouragement the frustrations and obstacles to producing this book and video would surely have gotten to me. Her belief in me and this project gave me the strength and motivation to fight the battles that blocked the path to success.

AUTHOR'S NOTE

Help! I Think I'm Dying! is a book which has no current equivalent in the mental health self-help market. It is unlike other trade books designed to help readers find solutions to the mental and emotional problems of panic attacks and phobias.

- It describes the different types of anxiety disorders.

- It gives readers the knowledge they need to assess their requirements for mental health services.

- It explains in laymen's terms the physiology and brain chemistry involved in these disorders.

- It describes the differences between psychiatrists, psychoanalysts, psychologists, social workers, counselors, psychiatric nurse practitioners and therapists.

- It analyzes and exposes some of the treatment abuses and misconceptions readers need to be aware of if they are to get the most for their mental health dollar.

- The glossary defines terminology readers might encounter and be confused by if they seek treatment. Use this reference anytime you come across a word you don't understand while reading this book.

- It allows readers to become educated consumers which will allow them to get the help they need to return to a normal, productive life.

INTRODUCTION
"Help! I Think I'm Dying!"

My eyes popped open. It was dark. The clock said 3:24 AM. I knew I was dying. I had severe crushing pain in the middle of my chest. I was having a heart attack even though I was only 36 years old. I was too young to die. I had too many things left to do. I had just started my psychiatric practice 4 years ago. It was a struggle driving 60 miles a day to three hospitals, my office and endless meetings. My wife and I had just purchased a lot and started our dream house. It took me every weekend for 2 years to clear it with a pick, shovel, chain saw and ax. We interviewed 11 architects, worked with three and had to sue one for taking us on a royal ride. We finally found an architect that designed the house we wanted and had broken ground 1 month ago.

All the sacrifices of time and energy put into studying in college to get the grades to get into medical school. All the sacrifices of time and energy studying in medical school to learn the art and science of medicine. All the sacrifices of time and energy taking call every fourth night in internship and residency with the 60, 70, 80 hours per week to refine the knowledge. Two years sacrifice of serving my country in the Army. Not now, after all the long, hard work and sacrifice of becoming a psychiatrist. I couldn't die now.

I checked my pulse. It was 90 beats per minute. My heart felt like it was going to jump out of my chest. I felt hot. I was sweating, and my fingers felt numb. My hands were shaking. I was so scared that I felt nauseous and thought I would vomit. My breathing was shallow and rapid. I had to get to the emergency room. I felt so dizzy. Time seemed to stand still. Everything was in slow motion.

I was sitting up in bed. My wife rolled over and asked me

what was wrong. I didn't want to scare her, so I told her I didn't feel well and was going out for a drive. I'd never done this before and she was both surprised and concerned, but I reassured her and told her to go back to sleep. I didn't want to die in front of her. I felt like a fool, and I didn't want her to see me like this. I quickly got dressed and drove to the hospital 5 minutes from my house. I left the car outside the emergency room door and ran in. I grabbed the first doctor I saw who happened to be a friend and told him to hook me up to an EKG. I was having a heart attack and was sure I was dying. We didn't even bother checking me in through admissions. He grabbed a nurse and had her help him set up the EKG. I felt a little relief that I had made it this far. At least if my heart stopped, there was a chance I could be revived.

My friend looked at the EKG. I was waiting to hear the bad news. He said it looked fine! What! There must be some mistake! The chest pain was now gone, and my heart rate was down to the low 80's, but I was still frightened out of my wits, and I knew I was dying. I asked him to recheck the EKG, and I asked to look at it. Again he said it was fine, and I could find no abnormality either.

What was going on? How could I be having a heart attack, know I was going to die and yet have a normal EKG? He suggested that I just lie back and relax, and he would continue to monitor me.

I began to feel embarrassed and foolish. I still felt frightened but the fear was beginning to subside. The numbness, dizziness, nausea had gone away. The only thing left was fear and that continued to subside.

My friend continued to check on me. He asked if I had been under any stress lately. Of course I had and explained the tar baby I was entangled in. He said that what I was experiencing was stress. There was nothing physically wrong with me. I argued how could that be. I was a psychiatrist and understood stress and its symptoms. Besides I had experienced lots of stresses in my life, and nothing ever felt like this did. The shame and embarrassment continued to grow until that made me feel uncomfortable enough to want to get out of there. It was 1½ hours later. The symptoms were gone, and I was no longer fearful that I was dying.

I went home. My wife was worried sick. She asked me what happened. I told her. She was bewildered that I would drive myself to the ER rather than letting her take me. What if I lost consciousness while driving?

I didn't want to listen to her logic and told her I was feeling okay now. Whatever it was, it was all over or so I thought.

I cut back on the 4-5 cups of coffee I was drinking each day figuring that I had to reduce my stress levels. I tried to spend a little less time at the new house, but there were always decisions to be made and problems to be solved. Fortunately, my practice slowed down a little, but that added a different kind of stress. How could I afford the house if I wasn't working full time? Well, I just wouldn't think about it. I would do my best and let the chips fall where they may.

I found it difficult to get to sleep. Somehow I became fearful that I would again awake in the middle of the night panicky. That never happened again.

Six weeks later, I was driving from my house to my first hospital to make rounds. It began to start all over again. The tightness in the chest. The severe chest pain, rapid heart beat, hot and sweaty, rapid and shallow breathing, numbness in my fingers, nausea. I knew I was going to die this time. I was 15 minutes away from the hospital in the middle of an expressway. I'd never make it. Slow motion returned.

I hoped I wouldn't accidently run my car into anyone else and hurt or kill them if I blacked out. I began to cry for fear of my wife and children having to get along without me. I knew I was going to die. But this is what had happened before, and there was nothing wrong with my heart. It was just stress.

I took my pulse, and although it was about 90 beats per minute, it was regular and strong. I had no pain in my left shoulder, neck, jaw or arm. The kind of pain that a heart attack generally causes. Could this be stress again? I sure didn't want to embarrass myself in front of my colleagues again.

By the time I got to the hospital, the overwhelming fear was gone. What remained was a less pervasive lingering fear. I put on the best mask I could and walked into the ER and asked one of the nurses to hook me up to an EKG. I told her I had a small bout of chest pain, and although I didn't think it was anything, I just wanted to make sure it wasn't. She looked concerned and hooked me up. After running the full EKG, she unhooked me and I read it. It looked okay to me. One of the ER doctors had come over to check me out. He reassured me the EKG was normal. I thanked them both and slowly walked to the doctors' lounge to think.

This was getting weird. I thought I must be going crazy. I couldn't live like this, but what could I do?

I decided to call a psychiatrist friend in Chicago. Maybe he could help explain what was happening to me. I called him that night and described the symptoms. He said, "You had two panic attacks probably brought on by all the stress you are under." I had never heard them called panic attacks. I had known them as anxiety attacks or hyperventilation syndrome. But the only symptoms were anxiety, a rapidly beating heart and hyperventilation. These were just beginning to be defined in the early 1980's with the new *DSM-III, Diagnostic and Statistical Manual of Mental Disorders*. This text was a major breakthrough in diagnosis because it clearly listed all the possible symptoms of each disorder. It described the usual age of onset of each illness and listed other illnesses which could mimic it. It made diagnosis more of a science than a guess, and it standardized the diagnosis of mental disorders.

Stress was too vague a term to grasp. So I got all the material I could relating to Panic Disorder and began to learn in depth about what I had experienced.

I began diagnosing, treating and understanding Panic Attacks, Panic Disorder and Phobias. Although I have since had several minor bouts of anxiety, fortunately I have never experienced another panic attack again.

My experience of having had two full blown panic attacks humbled me and sensitized me to the plight of those who have not been as fortunate as me and had just a few episodes of panic attacks. I became more understanding and compassionate to those who have numerous and more frequent panic attacks and have Panic Disorder and to those who have had Panic Disorder for a long enough period of time to have become phobic.

My experience of treating hundreds of patients since with varying degrees of this disorder from mild to severe and the recognition that it is too often misdiagnosed and inadequately treated and the fact that there is far too much misinformation given to the public has brought me to the point of writing this book. It is dedicated to all who suffer from one who truly understands.

Chapter 1

*"I Feel Different . . .
What's Going On?"*

Ralph is a healthy, physically fit, 27 year old, white male who began having panic attacks and anxiety five years ago.

He had his first panic attack after rigorous exercise. This progressed to getting panic attacks with mild exercise and sometimes even without exercise. His symptoms included hyperventilation, palpitations, "heart flutter," fear he was having a heart attack and was going to die, nausea, dizziness, hot and cold flashes, tremor, sweats, shortness of breath, feeling like he was choking, pressure in his chest and feeling that things around him looked and felt different.

Ralph went to his family doctor who did a complete medical exam which included a comprehensive cardiac work up. All tests came back negative.

He went to a psychiatrist who placed him on a benzodiazepine tranquilizer without explanation. Although the medication controlled his panic attacks, he felt uncomfortable taking the medication.

He then went to a psychologist for biofeedback. The psychologist told him this would help break his "addiction" to medication. He was able to stop the medication after several months, but his symptoms came back and would fluctuate with the stress in his life. His symptoms got progressively worse and finally got so bad that he was unable to carry on his normal physical routine. He underwent another complete medical and cardiac work up. These tests also came back negative.

Recently, job and social stresses increased his symptoms to the point that he reluctantly came to the conclusion that he needed psychiatric care and medication again in order to be able to function.

I diagnosed him as having panic attacks, originally brought on by exercise but later occurring spontaneously in any situation. His illness was discussed with him, and he was given a full explanation of how the medication worked. He reluctantly took the medication at first, but he recognized it kept his panic attacks under control. Each time we tried to stop his medication, his panic attacks returned.

He feels more comfortable taking his medication now and recognizes he will probably have to take medication for the rest of his life. He has desensitized to all previously feared situations and is currently able to do all he wants to do without restrictions.

At any six month period of time, some form of mental illness strikes 19% of the people living in the United States. Thirty-eight percent will experience a diagnosable mental illness within their lifetime. Yet, less than 5% will seek medical help of any kind, and less than 1% will seek mental health treatment of any kind.

Not recognizing what is wrong and not seeking proper treatment out of ignorance or fear causes those afflicted and their families unnecessary pain and suffering. It also costs businesses billions of wasted dollars in less productive employees, in unnecessary employee sick days and unnecessarily disabled employees.

Although more and more information is being presented in the media and in self-help books, most people avoid or ignore the information or are confused by it. Unfortunately, even if they seek out and study the information, much of that information will be inaccurate and contradictory. The public continues to receive an overabundance of misinformation about psychiatry and mental health care from the media: newspapers, magazines, movies and, particularly, television in the form of ever present talk show hosts looking for scandal with an eye on ratings rather than on education.

First, troubled people often avoid seeking help because they have an inaccurate perception of what their treatment may involve. Lying on the couch 3 to 5 times per week for years does not work for panic disorder. Being thrown into the "loony bin" or the "rubber room" or getting shock treatments is rare and is not necessary for most types of mental illnesses and not necessary at all for panic attacks and phobias.

Second, partly because of misinformation, too few people are aware that many disorders are now very treatable by a wide variety of medications in combination with less intensive talk therapies. Even those people who are knowledgeable about treatment may be wary of the social stigma attached to seeking treatment from the "crazy doctor" for "crazy behavior." Because of the existing social stigma, to admit they have gone into treatment with a psychiatrist, for whatever reason, makes them feel inappropriately weaker or less worthy than their family, friends or co-workers.

Third, people with emotional and behavioral problems

sometimes avoid getting the help they need because the system that provides that help can be both confusing and frightening. They are not sure how to find someone qualified to do an adequate evaluation and provide an accurate diagnosis and appropriate treatment. They often end up with poorly trained or marginally qualified help which preserves the myths that little can be done. Just understanding the skills and limitations of the different mental health care providers can be a monumental task. What is the difference between a psychiatrist, psychologist, social worker, counselor or psychiatric nurse? What about a psychoanalyst? Is he or she different from a psychotherapist?

Finally, the emotional immobility and emotional withdrawal created by the mental illness often makes it difficult for people to reach out for help in the first place. Seeking treatment may inappropriately lower their already low self-esteem.

If emotional or behavioral disorders are to be overcome or at least modified, people need a sufficient understanding of their condition. They need to overcome their fear of seeking help. And they need to know when, where and how to go about getting appropriate, cost effective help.

The general purpose of this book is to present in clear, non-technical, layman's terms a guide which will help the reader become aware of the progress that has been made over the past 30 to 40 years in understanding the nature of mental illness and the improvement in treatments. Specifically, it is a guide to help the reader understand in down-to-earth, understandable words what the mysterious afflictions called panic attacks and phobias really are and how they should be treated. It will explore the areas that puzzle people the most, including:

- What are the facts and fictions surrounding panic attacks and phobias?

- Where can qualified help be found?

4

- Do medications really work and, if so, why?

- Does treatment always require medication?

- How dangerous are medications? Are they addicting?

- Is there really any hope for someone suffering from panic attacks and phobias to return to a normal life?

This book can help you to use the mental health services available in your community to your best advantage. It will help you avoid the pitfalls of the system which could compound your problems and make them worse. It will also help you to:

- Identify symptoms of panic attacks and phobias.

- Understand the causes of panic attacks and phobias, so you can let go of the common myths and misconceptions surrounding them.

- Understand the kinds of treatments available to you.

- Recognize which treatments will be necessary and which will not be necessary for your condition.

- Be selective in choosing a mental health professional.

- Examine ways you can evaluate your therapist and your treatment.

- Understand words you might find confusing through use of the glossary.

You'll learn what you can expect from treatment, and the kinds of treatment that are appropriate and inappropriate for panic attacks and phobias. You'll learn how to tell if you are making progress or when you should look for a second opinion or change to another mental health professional.

Over the past forty years, major strides have been made in developing medications that can alter the course of many mental disorders. Medication therapies and short-term, talk therapies have been developed that decrease the time and expense of getting help. These treatments are very effective and have caused a revolution in the mental health field. They are similar to the discovery of penicillin to treat infection in general medicine.

If you or someone in your family seems to be having panic attacks and phobias, you need to be aware that effective help is available, and you need to know how to go about getting that help.

Chapter 2

Finding Someone To Help

Not so long ago, the symptoms of the most severe emotional and behavioral disorders were regarded as signs of demon possession or indications of personal or moral weakness. Until recently, people suffering from these disorders were hidden in attics or basements, were confined to institutions for most of their lives or had to suffer silently. Because over the centuries little could be done to alter the course of mental illness, misunderstanding, fear and stigma linger to this day.

Beginning in the 1930's, however, there were a number of revealing breakthroughs. Psychiatry began on the long journey of understanding how the brain functions to produce emotions and behaviors or malfunctions to produce emotional and behavioral disorders - mental illnesses.

In the 1930's, researchers first discovered neurotransmitters, chemicals in the brain that carry messages from one nerve to another. In the 1950's, chemists began to develop substances - medications - that helped to rebalance brain chemistry in people whose neurotransmitters were out of balance. By the 1970's, psychiatric researchers were just beginning to understand how these neurotransmitters affected thoughts, emotions and behaviors. Through the 1980's, the diagnostic categories were refined making the diagnosis and the study of the treatments more reliable. This produced treatments that were far more effective than at anytime in the past.

Far from being the result of weakness or faulty moral fiber, many emotional and behavioral disorders are traceable to a correctable malfunction of the brain cells.

There are, for example, research techniques that show the difference between the brain chemistry of a person suffering from panic attacks and phobias and the brain chemistry of a person whose brain is functioning normally. In fact, at this time, there are many scientific sign posts of genetic abnormalities associated with panic attacks, phobias and other common mental illnesses, such as depression, obsessive-compulsive disorder, attention deficit disorder, hyperactivity, just to name a few.

Although you may have experienced some of the symptoms that will be described in the following chapters, this does not necessarily mean that you are suffering from a mental disorder. You may just be identifying with and exaggerating the symptoms which are common and are experienced by most people at one time or another. For example, medical students typically begin to think they are afflicted with whatever disease they are studying. In addition, there may be other possible explanations for your experience. Even something as frightening as hallucinations can be produced by a lack of sleep, by taking too much of certain over-the-counter medications or by using street drugs. Furthermore, there are numerous medical and physical conditions which might create treatable mental disorders.

If you or a family member is experiencing these symptoms, you should consider getting a comprehensive evaluation so that you can find out what, if anything, is wrong.

Making an accurate diagnosis of a person experiencing emotional or behavioral changes is extremely complicated. There are many possible causes for most symptoms and few tests to help point the way to a foolproof diagnosis. The ability to diagnose accurately depends, to a great extent, on the background, education, training and experience of the person doing the evaluation. This makes psychiatry one of the most complex areas of the medical profession.

Even so, it is also the easiest field in which to fake competency. The mental health field started to become deregulated in the 1980's and is now filled with therapists with little or no training or therapists with varying degrees of training, equally competing with professionals with the highest, most comprehensive degrees of training. The public, insurance companies, the government and even many non-psychiatric medical doctors perceive the training of all mental health professionals to be equal. This is not so. The less the training the more likely the incompetence. It is always amusing to observe that the less training a therapist has the more he appears to look and dress like the stereotyped, media psychiatrist (three piece suit and a beard). The type of dress gives the appearance of credibility. However, looks can be and often are deceiving. The complexity of understanding the treatment field has become a mine field for the patient filled with inadequately, partially and poorly trained professionals and paraprofessionals. Watch where you step!

By becoming a knowledgeable consumer you become a wise consumer and are much more likely to avoid the pitfalls that deregulation has created. It's very easy for the therapist to hide behind technical terms that the patient doesn't understand, for the therapist to confuse patients with vague, imprecise terminology or for the therapist to say little or nothing in therapy and have the patient think he is getting help. You need to become familiar with your condition, its terminology and its proper treatment. This way you can become an informed consumer and avoid increasing your problems by getting incompetent, inappropriate or unnecessary help.

The brain is the organ that produces and regulates emotion and behavior. In trying to make a diagnosis, the brain must be viewed as a very sophisticated computer. In comparison, the most sophisticated, super computer produced today is a child's toy compared to the three pound computer we carry in our heads.

When evaluating the brain and trying to figure out what is

wrong with it, the diagnostician should see himself as a computer repairman. Before the computer can be fixed, the repairman has to find out what's wrong with it. In the same way, the diagnostician has to determine exactly what is wrong with the brain. A psychiatrist is uniquely qualified to do this. He should be looked upon as the most highly trained specialist in his field, rather than feared as the "madman" who will commit you to a hospital, lobotomize you, drug you up or take advantage of you. Seeing a board certified psychiatrist gives you your best chance for an accurate diagnosis and appropriate treatment.

Board certification means that the psychiatrist has successfully completed an approved psychiatric residency training program (4 years of psychiatric residency training after graduating from an approved 4 year medical school or osteopathic school) which makes him eligible to take the psychiatric "boards." At this point he is considered board eligible. He then has to pass the written examination before he is allowed to take the oral examination of the American Board of Psychiatry and Neurology. Once he passes the oral examination, he is board certified. This process takes at least 1½-2 years to complete after finishing residency.

Board certification is not necessary to practice psychiatry either in an office or in a hospital, and only about ⅔ of psychiatrists have become board certified. Board certification indicates a certain degree of confidence on the part of the psychiatrist and indicates a certain degree of his competence in the field of psychiatry.

Use your own judgment as to how well your psychiatrist is performing his job. There are many inadequately trained psychiatrists practicing today and board certification does not always eliminate them nor does it always guarantee excellence. Caution! There are many more inadequately trained counselors, social workers and psychologists. Excellence is often harder to find here. Regardless of the pitfalls of the training and certification process, a board certified psychiatrist is still the first person to start with when looking for treatment.

Before the psychiatrist can accurately diagnose a patient's problem, he has to first understand the kind of computer model the patient has inherited. He must understand the biological and chemical strengths and weaknesses of the equipment with which the patient was born.

Second, he has to analyze the programming of that computer: the behaviors, attitudes and responses that the patient has learned from his environment and his family. Although the major part of that programming occurs during the early years of life, programming continues to occur throughout life. As a result, people can learn to reprogram their computers, unlearn negative patterns of behavior and learn more constructive behaviors at any time in their lives. Talk therapy works here and helps speed up the healing process.

Finally, the psychiatrist has to understand the way a purely physical change in the brain may be affecting the patient's behavior. There may be an imbalance in the brain chemistry. This could be caused by psychological stress - faulty programming. It could be caused by situational stress - losing a job or the death of a close family member. It could be caused by physical stress - breaking a leg or dealing with an acute medical illness (the flu) or a chronic medical illness (arthritis). It could be caused directly by hundreds of medical conditions such as a brain tumor, liver disease, mercury poisoning, thyroid disease, just to list a few. See how complicated it can become?

To make an accurate diagnosis and treat a patient correctly, the psychiatrist has to know how and to what extent the genetics, the programming and the brain are affected and then try to determine the best way to repair the damaged parts. That's not always a simple or a quick task. Although an accurate diagnosis can usually be made in the first visit, it may take more than one visit.

The psychiatrist makes his diagnosis by taking a complete history from the patient. This would include the following:

IDENTIFYING DATA: Age, gender and race or cultural background of the patient.

CHIEF COMPLAINT: This is the main reason the patient has sought help and come to the psychiatrist.

PRESENT ILLNESS: This is a comprehensive history about the patient's chief complaint. It includes his symptoms and progression of symptoms. This history may include information from family, friends, medical records or other sources of information about the patient.

PAST HISTORY: This would include past episodes of the same chief complaint, the symptoms, length of time the symptoms lasted and any treatment given and the results of that treatment. In addition, past history would include any significant past medical problems, current medical problems and current medications being taken.

FAMILY HISTORY: This includes a history of any genetically related relatives who have had similar symptoms, their treatment and response to treatment.

DEVELOPMENTAL HISTORY: This includes where a person was born and raised, how many siblings he has, where he fits in the family, how he got along with parents and siblings, history of sexual or physical or emotional abuse, education, marriage, children and job.

MENTAL STATUS EXAM: This includes an assessment of the patient's: (1) judgment; (2) orientation to person, place and time; (3) insight into his illness and problems; (4) intellectual functioning; (5) memory; (6) affect; (7) thought content including delusions, hallucinations and suicidal thoughts; and (8) thought process or the ability of the patient to put thoughts together in a logical and goal directed manner.

After getting this information a diagnosis can be made and a treatment plan formulated.

Because each person is unique, each diagnosis presents a new challenge, a new opportunity to explore the complex interaction of mind and body. Just as fingerprints, bodies and faces are unique, so are brains, brain chemistry, programming, behaviors and emotions. Trying to find out what is causing a particular set of symptoms makes each patient an exciting, unsolved mystery for the psychiatrist.

Psychiatric nurse practitioners, counselors, social workers and psychologists don't have medical degrees and are therefore neither adequately trained to make an accurate diagnosis nor to establish an effective treatment plan. They can neither prescribe medications nor order laboratory tests. Senator Daniel Inouye chairs the Senate Defense Sub-Committee. This Sub-Committee put together an experiment to give psychologists a six month course in psychopharmacology and then allows them to prescribe psychotropic medications. They are going to practice on an unsuspecting group, active duty military personnel and their families. It has been suggested to this Sub-Committee that if they think this is such a great idea, they should allow these psychologists to practice on the Sub-Committee members and their families. They have ignored that suggestion. It doesn't take a genius to understand why!

There is a place for these mental health paraprofessionals in the treatment process, but it should not be at the top of the diagnostic and treatment pyramid where they are often found. They should work in conjunction with and under the supervision of a psychiatrist who should be leading and directing treatment. This is rarely done today. Deregulation allows these mental health paraprofessionals to practice independently.

Licensed clinical psychologists are as well trained as psychiatrists to do various types of talk therapy. They are usually better trained than psychiatrists to administer and interpret psychological tests. Psychological testing is not magical and is ordered far more often than necessary. If it is ordered for you, make sure you understand why and make sure you agree with the reasoning. It is costly.

Licensed clinical social workers are not as well trained as psychologists or psychiatrists to do talk therapy. They are competent to do talk therapy in uncomplicated cases, provide family therapy and act as co-therapists in groups.

Licensed professional counselors are the least trained of the licensed therapists. They should do talk therapy in only the simplest of cases and can act as co-therapists in groups.

Because diagnosis determines treatment, it is important that you get diagnosed as accurately as possible. Start with a board certified psychiatrist. You wouldn't want your family doctor to diagnose your heart condition. You would want to go to a cardiologist, the specialist in his field. You wouldn't have a general surgeon remove a brain tumor. You would go to a neurosurgeon.

A psychiatrist is the only medical doctor who specializes in mental health. He is also the only mental health professional who is a medical doctor. He is the specialist in his field. A board certified psychiatrist has proven his competency by passing the psychiatric specialty boards. He is the person most qualified to give you an accurate diagnosis and recommend appropriate treatment. However, just as there are excellent, average and poor quality doctors of every specialty, so too, there are excellent, average and poor quality psychiatrists. This book should help you to find psychiatrists of excellence and should help you avoid psychiatrists practicing average or poor quality psychiatry in regard to panic attacks and phobias.

In today's climate of deregulation and managed care, psychiatric nurse practitioners, counselors, social workers and psychologists are able to practice independently without psychiatric supervision - to diagnose and treat on their own! This is an accident waiting to happen, and it often does even though the patient might not be aware of it.

In some instances, however, the paraprofessionals may work in a group headed by a psychiatrist. If you go to such a group, be sure that the psychiatrist does the initial evaluation and diagnosis and then supervises the treatment. Often, for the group's financial reasons, the practitioner with the first opening in his or her schedule will be the one to do the initial evaluation, and there will be very little, if any, ongoing psychiatric supervision. A psychiatrist with a large staff of paraprofessionals can make a lot more money than one working alone or one working with a few paraprofessionals.

Often psychologists, social workers or counselors put together large groups of mental health providers. They may have a psychiatrist in the group as a "consultant" or as an employee. The presence of the psychiatrist gives them the appearance of credibility. Don't be fooled by appearances. Use extreme caution when going to the large mental health groups!

Don't go to or call a psychiatric hospital for a referral to a psychiatrist. The psychiatric hospitals spend staggering amounts of money advertising for patients with the promise of a free evaluation. They ask you to call their 24 hour crisis line or brag about their specialty programs for children, depression, panic disorder, alcohol, drug abuse, etc. Remember, hospitals make money by filling beds. Often patients are unnecessarily hospitalized and remain inappropriately hospitalized until insurance coverage runs out. The largest national psychiatric hospital chain was investigated by the Justice Department and criminally prosecuted for these types of abuses. They were made to divest themselves of their psychiatric hospitals and fined over $350 million. This was the single largest corporate fine in the history of the United States.

Often in the HMO (Health Maintenance Organization) "managed care" settings, the family doctor makes the psychiatric diagnosis and prescribes the medication and then refers the patient to a counselor, social worker or psychologist for the talk therapy. The family doctor is poorly trained to do so. He may have had 2 to 4 months of experience during his psychiatric rotation in medical school. He may have had brief psychiatric encounters in internship and have had a few more in residency. He may later have taken a 1 day or a 1 week postgraduate, continuing medical education course in psychiatry. This does give him some knowledge about psychiatry but does not qualify him to practice psychiatry. I delivered 29 babies during my 2 month obstetrics rotation in medical school. This does not qualify me to practice obstetrics.

A family doctor plus a counselor, a social worker or a psychologist is a case of the partially blind leading the partially blind. They can each see a little bit but getting from point A to point B becomes hazardous for the patient. If the patient is not an educated consumer, he might think he is getting the best help that is available. Certainly his employer, his insurance company, his HMO, his family doctor and his therapist are not going to tell him differently. They all have a financial stake at delivering the **least** expensive care possible not the highest quality care possible. They might even sincerely believe, through their own bias and lack of training, that they are delivering the best care possible. Most often they are not.

These are some of the major pitfalls in the system as currently practiced in the United States today, and it looks like it is going to get worse. The government wants the general practitioners and family doctors to do most of the diagnosis and treatment because they cost less than the specialists. Watch out! You get what you pay for!

Studies show that 60 to 70% of **all** non-psychiatric medical visits are related to some form of mental disorder. Non-psychiatric physicians diagnose about 50% of these patients correctly. That means they miss about 50% of the diagnosis. Further, only half of the patients who are diagnosed correctly are put on medications that provide some symptomatic relief but get no form of talk therapy. This means that at least 75%, if not more, of patients seeing non-psychiatric MD's are being misdiagnosed and mistreated for mental disorders! This not only increases the cost of medical treatment but can also be very dangerous. It can prolong the illness and make it worse.

> A patient who had chest pains was afraid she was having a heart attack. Referred to a local hospital emergency room by the walk-in clinic, she was admitted to the Coronary Care Unit. Her lab tests were normal. She was referred to another hospital for X-ray studies of her coronary arteries. During this procedure, one coronary artery was accidentally ruptured requiring emergency open chest surgery to prevent her from dying. She was told that this procedure had corrected the problem causing her chest pains.

> Two months later, when her symptoms returned, she went to another doctor who thought she might be having panic attacks and referred her to me. She had classic symptoms of panic disorder. After appropriate treatment, she is in full remission, is off medications and no longer requires treatment. The toughest part of treating her was dealing with her anger at her initial medical doctors who missed the correct

diagnosis of panic disorder and almost killed her.

One third of all patients referred for X-ray studies of their coronary arteries have normal findings but meet all the criteria for a diagnosis of panic disorder.

General practitioners, internists and gynecologists often prescribe psychotropics - medications that affect the mind. As a group, they currently prescribe more benzodiazepine tranquilizers (Valium, Xanax, etc.) than psychiatrists, and most of these non-psychiatric physicians are not well-schooled in the fine points in the use of these medications.

Taking medication prescribed by a doctor who is not fully aware of how the medication works or of its potential side effects is never wise. Medications need to be carefully monitored and adjusted. Seek a second opinion if your problem isn't getting better within 2 months.

There are several different schools of psychiatry: 1) biological psychiatry, which minimizes talk therapy but uses a variety of brief, short-term talk therapies and leans heavily toward medication therapies (psychopharmacology); 2) general psychiatry, which includes a variety of talk therapies and medication therapies; and 3) psychoanalysis, which leans heavily toward intensive, long-term talk therapy and avoids or limits medication therapy.

If medication is indicated, you need to look for a psychiatrist who is a psychopharmacologist - a psychiatrist who is an expert in the use of the psychiatric medications. Most biological psychiatrists are psychopharmacologists, but not all psychiatrists are experts in the use of these medications. Some are trained to do mostly talk therapy and are poorly trained in the use of medications. Some are trained in the fine points of the use of medications but are poorly trained to do talk therapy.

You need to find a psychiatrist who is well trained to do both. Board certification can help here because it tests for competence in talk therapy in addition to competence in medication therapy. Ask your psychiatrist about his training, experience and competency in both talk therapy and medication therapy.

Some psychiatrists are trained as psychoanalysts. They believe that all mental illness is caused by faulty, learned behavior or emotion and that analyzing the patient will lead to a correction of that behavior or emotion. While this technique may help you understand yourself better, it rarely produces the promised cure. Most people can't afford the time or money (3 - 5 sessions per week at $80 - $200 per session which can continue for years) to get this treatment in the first place. It is an older treatment technique which is useful in certain cases but should be used in a limited fashion. There are still far too many psychiatrists practicing psychoanalysis today. Old habits are hard to break, and there is still far too much credence given to psychoanalysis. Even though the use of psychiatric medications isn't being taught in psychoanalytical training programs, the psychoanalytic idea that we shouldn't use medications because they mask the "real" problem still hangs like a dark cloud over the psychiatric and mental health profession. After all, if mental illness is caused by genetic imbalances in brain chemistry and can be corrected by medications, psychoanalysts are out of business! Too few psychoanalysts want to go back to school and be brought up-to-date in knowledge and treatment. This causes psychoanalysis to be over prescribed.

Remember, you are the health care consumer, and it is your responsibility to see that you are getting your money, time and effort's worth. You need to take charge of your life and the lives of family members who are too young, too sick, too confused or too old to combat the system. Being an informed consumer gives you the knowledge and, therefore, the power to get effective treatment.

If you have doubts about your diagnosis or treatment, you need to ask questions until you understand the diagnosis and agree with the treatment plan. If things are still not clear, change to another psychiatrist.

Panic attacks and phobias are very treatable. In most cases, with proper treatment, you should be able to return to your normal life and do everything you used to be able to do in a relatively short time.

> Rita is a 26 year old, white female. She began having panic attacks in high school after trying to deliver a report in front of the class. She couldn't finish and had to sit down. Fearful of ever getting into that situation again, she became very clever at devising ways to avoid these situations.
>
> She wanted to go to college but was too fearful to even try it. She found a job that allowed her to avoid interacting with others. Being very bright, she continued to get promoted and finally achieved a level, as an insurance adjuster, where she not only had to deal with the public but also had to supervise other employees. She felt very uncomfortable.
>
> She went to a psychologist who treated her with desensitization for two and one half months. It seemed to help initially, but soon her symptoms started to get worse again. She next went to her GP who put her on medication that had no effect. She quit the medication after three weeks.
>
> The panic attacks increased to the point that she was on the verge of quitting her job when she came to me for help. She was fearful she

was going crazy.

I explained her condition to her and told her how we were going to conquer it. I urged her not to quit her job but to hang on until we could get her panic under control.

I put her on medications that worked very rapidly for her at low doses. I taught her how to desensitize, and she was able to accomplish this quickly on her own. She now feels comfortable doing anything her job requires of her. She still takes medication and after only one year of treatment started coming in for monthly, med-check visits.

She recently felt comfortable enough to start applying for higher job positions but most required a college degree. She decided to give it a try and first took one college course. After breezing through it and getting an A, she began taking 2 to 3 courses at a time while still working. She is now on her way to achieving her college degree. She will soon be in a position to start climbing the corporate ladder.

For some patients it may take longer. Don't give up; perseverance pays off. Trying different treatments, medications or therapists may add another step on the road to recovery. The road may be a short one or could be a long and treacherous one, but it will have an end. Recovery does not necessarily mean cure. It generally means taking maintenance medication and getting maintenance talk therapy for your lifetime. However, this will allow you to live your life normally again.

June was 21 when she had her first panic attack. She was happily married, was the proud mother of a beautiful, eight month old, baby girl and recently began working at a good job. Everything was going great for her when suddenly, without warning, she began to have difficulty taking a deep breath, her chest felt heavy, her scalp felt tight, her hands began tingling, her heart began pounding. She became fearful it would burst out of her chest. She felt like she was dying. She felt like she was outside her body watching herself. She couldn't tell anybody, fearful they would think she was crazy.

June ended up in the emergency room where the doctors ran some tests on her. The tests were normal and the doctors told her there was nothing physically wrong with her. They gave her tranquilizers, but the symptoms persisted and she gradually began to develop many phobias.

She became fearful of closed in spaces. She couldn't eat at restaurants. She couldn't go to the grocery store and wait in line or write a check. She became so fearful of driving that she stopped driving and even became fearful of riding in a car.

Her family and her first husband didn't understand what was wrong with her and gave her no support. She quit working and became house bound for two years. Her husband couldn't take it anymore and divorced her.

She mustered all her strength and forced herself out of necessity to go out of the house and work for the next ten years. The attacks went through cycles. There were long periods where she felt good and other times when the attacks became frequent and severe. She suffered through them.

She married again at age 32. The attacks returned and she couldn't control them. They became so severe she became house bound again. This time it lasted five years. Finally June's internist referred her to me.

After a complete medical work-up to rule out physical causes for her problems, she was placed on a variety of medications.

Talk therapy didn't reveal any causes for her symptoms. Medications were adjusted, changed and combined but we could only achieve 60 - 70% symptom relief.

Finally after five years, June was convinced to try an MAO inhibitor. Within 3 months she was completely panic attack free and was able to desensitize from all her phobias. She has remained in remission since 1986. She continues to take her medication and sees me every three months for medication checks.

June has been able to regain her life and is living it the way she chooses to live it.

Chapter 3

The Anxiety Disorders

Anxiety disorders, which include panic attacks and phobias, are one of the most common psychiatric conditions today affecting 7% of the population. The distress they cause ranges from butterflies in the stomach to terror so intense that life becomes unbearably frightening. There are many people in this country who are prisoners in their own homes because the fear they feel when they leave home becomes physically incapacitating (agoraphobia). There are other people for whom supermarkets, churches, restaurants, shopping malls or crowded theaters - places where they have experienced panic attacks - have become off limits. Very few people who have not experienced panic attacks or other related disorders first-hand or second-hand can imagine the extent to which they can cripple and even snuff out the joy of life. Fortunately, these conditions are very treatable if appropriate combinations of medication therapies and talk therapies are applied. Becoming familiar with the diagnostic categories and symptoms for each category can help lead you to an accurate diagnosis.

PANIC DISORDER

Panic disorder is characterized by recurrent panic attacks. Having one or several panic attacks does not constitute panic disorder. This could be the early stage of panic disorder and could progress to more frequent panic attacks or could stop with no more panic attacks. In order to be diagnosed as having panic disorder, an individual must have at least four panic attacks within a four week period, or the attacks must be followed by the fear of having another attack. As you can see, the criteria are somewhat arbitrary. Because emotions are variable, panic attacks can vary from light to very severe, and the frequency can vary from infrequent to almost continuous. Generally, an individual will experience any or all of the following symptoms during a panic attack:

- Shortness of breath or feelings of smothering

- Dizziness, unsteady feelings, faintness or light-headedness

- Choking sensations, difficulty swallowing, feeling your throat is closing or feeling something is caught in your throat

- Palpitations - feeling your heart is beating so hard and fast that it is going to jump out of your chest

- Increased heart rate

- Trembling or shaking

- Abdominal distress including cramping, nausea, vomiting or diarrhea

- Numbness or tingling sensations especially of the hands and feet but also of the head or face

- Hot flashes or chills

- Severe, crushing chest pains with the feeling that you are having a heart attack and that you are going to die

- Fear that you are dying

- Fear that you are going crazy or you are going to lose control of yourself and go berserk, make a fool of yourself or embarrass yourself

- Blurred vision

- Headache

- Derealization - feelings of unreality, things around you don't appear real, things might look different or feel different, time seems to slow down and everything appears to be in slow motion, sounds might get louder or softer even though you know the intensity is not changing, objects might appear brighter or duller, or might appear larger or smaller even though you know the object is not changing

- Depersonalization - feeling that you are outside your body looking back at it, or feeling like your arms or legs are detached from your body or like they belong to someone else

The attacks usually occur suddenly with the intense feeling of fear, panic, dread or impending doom. Sometimes there is a feeling that an attack is building. They occur when there is no real environmental cause to panic and appear "out of the blue." They usually last several minutes (2-10) with a less severe discomfort lasting hours. The severe panic can sometimes last hours or days, but this is rare. Very often, the first attack occurs when smoking marijuana, using cocaine, amphetamines or excess caffeine. They can also be caused by hyperthyroidism, adrenaline-producing tumors, insulin-producing tumors or other medical conditions. This type should go away without return after the abused drug is discontinued or the medical condition is corrected. Sometimes the abused drug or medical condition sensitizes a person to have panic attacks which continue as panic disorder after the abused drug is discontinued or the medical condition is corrected.

Panic disorder usually begins in the mid to late 20's but can begin in childhood or old age. It is slightly more common in women than men.

Once panic attacks begin, they generally come in clusters of increasing frequency. They can spontaneously disappear for an extended period of time only to return later with increased intensity and frequency.

Some researchers believe that a sudden loss in childhood predisposes one to panic attacks in adulthood. Others don't agree. The more common environmental thread appears to be increased stress which can be experienced in childhood or experienced at any time in life. Stress in combination with genetic abnormalities are the most likely predisposing factors. They prevent areas of the brain from producing enough neurotransmitters to keep the brain chemistry properly balanced and functioning normally.

PANIC DISORDER WITH PHOBIAS

Panic disorder with phobias has the same symptoms as panic disorder with the addition of phobias. These first start as anticipatory anxiety where the individual develops a fear of places or situations where he has previously experienced a panic attack. This leads to phobic avoidance behavior - avoiding those places or situations whenever possible. If left untreated, it leads to phobias - avoiding those places or situations no matter what or experiencing a great deal of discomfort if forced to remain there.

Any place or any situation can cause phobias to develop, but they generally develop to the more common situations and places in which people find themselves. These are usually places and situations where people feel trapped, where escape would be difficult, where medical help would be hard to obtain or where fleeing would produce embarrassment.

Some people confine themselves to the only genuinely safe place they know, their home. This is called agoraphobia. Others might venture away from home but might require a "safe person" to accompany them. A "safe person" is someone who understands and accepts their condition and will return them home no matter what or will make sure medical help will be provided if necessary. Others will drive or go places alone but only in their "safe area" which is usually a very short distance from their home. Sometimes they require their "safe person" to remain home with them or be readily available should the need arise.

Some may be able to force themselves to endure the attacks. They may learn to endure the severe anxiety and go where they need to or do what they have to at the cost of a great deal of discomfort. Rarely, some may desensitize enough that the panic attacks subside to a tolerable level or disappear.

The most common phobias include fear of bridges, tunnels, expressways, traveling outside of a perceived safe distance from home, fear of elevators, heights, shopping malls, grocery stores, theaters, restaurants, crowded areas, standing in line, stopping in traffic, writing a check in public, traveling in a train, bus or airplane, getting a haircut or going to the dentist or doctor.

SPECIFIC OR SIMPLE PHOBIA

Specific phobia is a chronic, unrealistic or excessive fear of one certain object or situation, such as a fear of dogs, spiders, snakes, mice, flying, elevators, closed spaces, heights, thunderstorms, water, medical procedures - such as having blood taken, injections, operations, fear of injury or dental work. The individual will experience intense anxiety or panic when faced with the feared object or situation and may experience some of the same symptoms of panic disorder. However, the symptoms only occur when faced with the feared object or situation, and the intensity of symptoms is directly proportional to the closeness of the feared object or situation. An individual can force himself to remain in contact with the object or stay in the situation at the expense of a great deal of discomfort. Generally, he will do his best to avoid these circumstances. In addition, the individual will recognize that the fear is unrealistic and is blown way out of proportion to the circumstance.

Most specific phobias start in childhood and disappear in time without treatment. If they continue into adulthood, most individuals will avoid the circumstance and not seek treatment. Treatment is effective in people whose specific phobias create problems in their daily living.

POST TRAUMATIC STRESS DISORDER

Post traumatic stress disorder occurs when an individual is involved in or witnesses a catastrophic event or situation where death, threatened death or severe injury is experienced. Examples are war, earthquake, tornado, hurricane, auto accident, plane crash, accidental death of a family member or friend, rape, torture, etc. Almost anyone experiencing the same catastrophe would react in a similar way with extreme fear, panic, terror or helplessness. The person will continue to relive the catastrophe in his mind or have flashbacks to the event upon waking from sleep or when drinking alcohol. He will try to avoid anything which reminds him of the catastrophe. He may unconsciously protect himself either by feeling numb to all life events or by becoming hypersensitized and anxious to all life events. Frequently, he will experience recurrent nightmares about the catastrophe. Symptoms usually start right after the catastrophic experience but can show up months or years later.

Other symptoms include:

- Attempts at avoiding thoughts, feelings, activities, places, situations, people or any sort of communication about or memory of the event

- Memory lapses about details of the event

- Decreased interest in participating in any events

- Decreased interest in interacting with others, in addition to social withdrawal

- Decreased ability to make long term plans including a sense that the future does not exist or is unimportant

- Difficulty sleeping

- Short tempered, irritable, angry

- Easily startled

- Difficulty focusing one's attention or concentrating

GENERALIZED ANXIETY DISORDER

Generalized anxiety disorder occurs when an individual experiences exaggerated anxiety or worry about many events and situations which is out of proportion to the events or situations. The anxiety or worry can persist for months or years and is present most of the time. Symptoms can include:

- Trembling, twitching, feeling shaky

- Headache

- Muscle tension, soreness or aching especially of the head, neck and back

- Feeling restless or hyped up

- Tiring easily

- Difficulty getting to sleep or staying asleep

- Difficulty focusing one's attention or concentrating

- Forgetfulness

- Irritability

- Plus all of the symptoms of panic disorder except the panic or terror

Chapter 4

Panic Attacks

The words panic attack are very descriptive for the disorder that causes episodes of sheer terror. The acute episode usually lasts several minutes, but this brief time seems like an eternity. The following less intense feelings from the attack can linger hours to days with feelings of confusion, discomfort and apprehension.

These attacks occur spontaneously and unexpectedly in situations that would not normally produce panic or anxiety. They come "out of the blue." As the illness progresses and more panic attacks occur, feelings of anticipatory anxiety begin - apprehension when getting into a situation similar to one where a panic attack has occurred before. This leads to phobic avoidance behavior - avoiding these places and situations whenever possible. If left untreated, it finally leads to phobias - avoiding these places and situations no matter what or experiencing a great deal of discomfort if forced to remain in that situation.

A panic attack usually starts with the sudden onset of intense apprehension, fear, terror or the feeling of impending doom. Any or all of the following may be experienced:

- Hyperventilation (shallow rapid breathing), shortness of breath or feelings of smothering

- Dizziness, unsteady feelings or feeling you are going to faint

- Choking sensations, difficulty swallowing, feeling your throat is closing or that something is caught in your throat

- Palpitations - strong, rapid heartbeats with the feeling your heart is going to jump out of your chest

- Increased heart rate

- Trembling or shaking

- Abdominal distress including cramping, nausea, vomiting or diarrhea

- Numbness or tingling sensations especially of the hands and feet but also of the head or face

- Hot flashes or chills

- Sweating

- Severe, crushing chest pain with feelings that you are going to have a heart attack and die

- Fear that you are dying

- Fear that you are going crazy, you are going to lose control of yourself and go berserk, make a fool of yourself or embarrass yourself

- Derealization – Feelings of unreality in relation to the environment. Things around you don't appear real. Time seems to slow down and everything appears to be in slow motion. Things might look different or feel different; sounds might get louder or softer even though you know the intensity is not changing. Objects might appear brighter and duller or might appear larger or smaller even though you know the object is not changing.

- Depersonalization - Feelings of unreality related to one's self. Feeling that you are outside your body looking back at it, or feeling like your arms or legs are detached from your body or belong to someone else.

During the first few panic attacks, you will probably seek emergency medical care. Often the emergency room doctor or family doctor doesn't recognize or correctly diagnose the condition. You may be admitted to a hospital and be put through a number of expensive tests or be run through the tests as an outpatient. When all the tests come up negative, the doctors are stumped. They might tell you it is just stress.

Since the condition usually starts slowly with panic attacks occurring infrequently, the doctor might tell you that since all tests have come out normal, there is nothing physically wrong with you. You are fine and there is no reason to worry. You know he has missed something terribly wrong with you, but you start to doubt yourself. When the next attack occurs, you again go to the emergency room or your doctor. Again you get the tests, and they all come out normal. Again he tells you it is stress or anxiety and there is nothing wrong with you. You know he has missed something that is going to kill you. But he is the doctor, and you begin to doubt yourself even more and think that you really are going crazy. Finally, out of embarrassment and feeling that you are making a nuisance of yourself, you stop going to the doctor and begin to suffer the agony of the attacks alone or with a trusted spouse, family member or friend. You start to get depressed.

Your doctor might have even suggested you see a psychiatrist. This adds fuel to the fire that even he thinks you are crazy or it's all in your head and you are making it up.

You won't see a psychiatrist because you fear what people will think, but out of desperation, you see a psychologist, social worker or counselor. After all, if you see one of them, you're not crazy or as sick. Besides it costs less and your insurance company has referred you to one who participates in their program. Your panic attacks continue. You are now afraid to drive alone or go to the grocery store. You can't wait in line or write a check. If you have one of these dreaded attacks with a basket full of groceries, you can't just leave them and run for the door. People will definitely label you as crazy. If you try to write a check in front of the cashier, everyone in line will see your hands shaking and the sweat pouring down your face. You stop going to the grocery store and find excuses to have others go for you. You stop going to church because even sitting in the last row on the aisle still makes you uncomfortable. You stop going to the mall because everyone there can see the terror in your eyes and knows you are crazy. You are convinced you will vomit in your plate if you go to a restaurant, so you stop going out to eat. Soon you find you can't even get a haircut without feeling trapped in the chair. You put off dental exams because there is no way you can control yourself trapped in the dental chair with a dental pick and a saliva suction tube in your mouth and the dentist hovering over your face. You stop going out with friends. You find excuses not to visit them and stop asking them to visit you. Vacations which include airplanes, trains, buses or long car trips are out of the question.

It seems as though the walls are closing in, and you find it difficult driving through a tunnel, on a bridge or on an expressway. What if you have one of these terrifying attacks and become trapped? Surely you will go stark, raving mad! But the doctors said it was stress. It was all in your head. There is nothing physically wrong with you. You become fearful of riding in a car more than two miles, then one mile, then two blocks from your home. Finally, you are trapped in the only safe place you have found, your house. You may find that alcohol gives you temporary relief, so you start to self-medicate with it and may start to abuse alcohol and even become an alcoholic. Your depression intensifies.

You can force yourself to go to the therapist with your "safe person," someone who will bring you back home no matter what or will make sure medical help is provided should you have one of these attacks outside your home. The therapist is teaching you relaxation therapy. That helps a little, but that nagging, gnawing feeling eats away at you. He tells you the panic attacks won't kill you or harm you. You have to force yourself to do the things you dread the most. It's helping. You can get into the car and do some of the things that you weren't able to do before. If you have a panic attack, he teaches you to do deep breathing exercises, to focus your attention on other things around you or to snap a rubber band on your wrist. You start counting ceiling tiles, telephone poles or light bulbs. Sometimes you seem to be spending hours counting. You are able to do more and get out of the house more, but the attacks are still painful even though you have learned to cope with them to some extent. You still can't fully return to your former life. This is the best it can get, but life is no longer fun. Most of your time and energy is spent worrying about the next attack or dealing with the current one. You feel hopeless, helpless, withdrawn, depressed and alone.

Your therapist may even refer you to a family doctor or an internist he works with to get medication. You try to take the medication but fear becoming addicted to it. Your doctor tells you he can only prescribe the medication for several months because it is dangerous. He tries several medications, but the side effects are intolerable. They make you "zombied out." You can't function on them. Besides, they don't work very well. You stop taking them. You begin to doubt your doctor and therapist. Do they really know what they are doing? If they do, why are you not feeling better? Is there any hope of regaining your life?

Life has become a nightmare. Your family doesn't understand and is very angry with you. You have lost most of your friends. "Just be strong, ignore it, don't worry so much, get on with your life like everyone else," they tell you. You have spent lots of money on treatment, and this is the best it is going to get. You read everything you can get your hands on about panic attacks. They reaffirm that the treatment you are getting is correct, and you are doing as well as can be expected, or they confuse you, they are hard to understand and you find them contradictory. With all the confusion and misinformation about panic attacks, medications and psychiatry, it is no wonder that most people don't get proper treatment or get poor quality, partial treatment.

The good news is that help is available and effective. You can get your full life back, and it won't cause you to get a third mortgage on your home, to sell your kids or to get locked up in the "loony bin." You might have to make small financial sacrifices at the beginning of treatment, but the cost decreases as you improve and become stabilized. Insurance has been paying a smaller share of the cost of mental health treatment over the past decade. You will find that you have to pay a larger share out of pocket for that treatment. You will have to decide what is more important - material things or regaining your health and once again being able to enjoy your life to the fullest. You will often find that proper treatment will more than pay for itself as you become more productive and your ability to earn increases.

George, a 40 year old, white male, experienced panic attacks and phobias since his twenties. He smoked marijuana and used LSD on numerous occasions. He had his first panic attack while smoking marijuana. Although he continued to use marijuana, he didn't enjoy it because of the anxiety it produced. During a sunny afternoon while on LSD, things around him stopped looking real.

George stopped using street drugs but continued to experience panic attacks that waxed and waned for no apparent reason. He was artistically inclined and began painting pictures. Not being able to make a living at this, he became a contractor for minor housing renovations.

He was able to make a modest living, but the increasing frequency of panic attacks led to phobias. He became fearful of riding in a car or a truck with fellow workers. He was fearful that if he had a panic attack, they would see it. If he asked to be let out of the car or truck, he was fearful they would laugh at him or think he was a "sissy." He experienced increasing difficulty working with anyone else on any project. He declined more and more work and finally fell into a working arrangement with a friend. They would buy a run-down house. He would do all the work on it to bring it up to saleable standards. The friend would then sell the house, and they would split the profits equally.

He came to my office at the end of his rope just squeaking by on a near poverty level income. He was desperate to get over these frightening attacks but fearful he could not afford private treatment. He refused to go to the Community Mental Health Center to get publicly funded treatment.

I told him if he came in for regular treatment and followed the treatment recommendations, not only would he be able to afford the private care, but he would also substantially improve his income. In other words, the treatment would more than pay for itself. I told him he could pay for a small portion of his treatment at the time of each visit, and he could pay off the difference after he got back on his feet emotionally and economically.

He was suspicious and reluctant to take me up on my recommendations, but desperation won the day. We started talk therapy and medication therapy and soon had his symptoms of panic under control. By the end of the first year of treatment, he was able to get rid of the "friend," hire a helper and began soliciting for work independently.

He still experiences some visual illusions and distortions (derealization) on bright sunny days, but he is able to do anything he wants. His income has more than tripled, and he has finally come to terms with his illness.

The first year of treatment cost him about four thousand dollars for both therapy and medications. Maintenance therapy and medication now costs him about five hundred dollars per year. He is very satisfied with the progress he has made, and we continue to work toward full remission of symptoms. He recognizes that the visual illusions and distortions might be a permanent side effect of LSD use, but, hopefully, we will one day find a solution to that last vestige of his illness.

Panic attacks are a physical malfunction of the brain. There is a genetic predisposition for them. In other words, this condition runs in families although most affected family members do their best to hide it from each other because of the stigma of the illness and their lack of understanding about it. There are probably a dozen or more genes that can predispose you to panic attacks. If you inherit one of those genes and if enough stress, either physical or psychological or a combination of both, hits you at one time, it triggers the gene into action. You then have panic attacks. For a lucky few this can be temporary. It may only last weeks, months or years – then go away never to return. For most it becomes progressive and worsens with time and becomes panic disorder.

Sometimes panic attacks can be triggered by excess caffeine. I have seen patients who were drinking 4 to 10 cups of coffee a day in addition to drinking iced tea or drinking caffeinated soft drinks and taking over-the-counter medications containing caffeine. They were ingesting large amounts of caffeine. This was causing their panic attacks. All they had to do was to stop all caffeine. Their panic attacks went away and required no further treatment.

When caffeine is abruptly stopped, caffeine withdrawal occurs. It starts within 24 hours of the last dose of caffeine and usually lasts 3 to 5 days. You will experience a severe, dull, throbbing headache that does not respond to pain medication. You will also feel weak and sluggish. But it will go away and going through caffeine withdrawal is a lot easier to tolerate than panic attacks.

Often the general practitioner, internist or cardiologist will make the diagnosis of prolapsed mitral valve, a stretching of the heart valve between the heart chambers on the left side of the heart. This was once thought to produce panic-like symptoms. However, more thorough research has shown prolapsed mitral valve to be nothing more than a variation of normal. A small percentage of people have prolapsed mitral valve. Most have no symptoms at all. Most people with panic attacks have nothing wrong with their heart valves. There are a few who have both panic attacks and prolapsed mitral valve, but these conditions are independent of each other.

A diagnosis of panic attacks supposedly being caused by a prolapsed mitral valve is an example of the general practitioner's, internist's and cardiologist's reluctance to recognize mental illness, of their own fear of mental illness, of their lack of being fully knowledgeable about panic disorder or of their inability to keep up with the fast-paced advances of knowledge in all medical fields. This is one reason why psychiatrists, specialists in mental health, are needed.

Hypoglycemia (low blood sugar) is another common example of misdiagnosis and the need for psychiatrists. This is often diagnosed as the cause of panic attacks and anxiety. However, it is an extremely rare condition and only produces apprehension, sweating, tremor and palpitations. These symptoms only occur when the blood sugar goes below a certain level. Eating a piece of candy or drinking a glass of orange juice will make the symptoms go away immediately. In order to make a diagnosis of hypoglycemia, your doctor must have you eat a lot of sweets for 3 days before he does a 5 hour glucose tolerance test on you. This is a blood test to check your blood sugar levels. You are required to fast for 12 hours before you drink a sweet drink with a standard amount of glucose (sugar) in it. Blood is drawn prior to drinking the sweet drink, ½ hour later and then every hour for five hours. This blood is analyzed for the amount of glucose (sugar) in it. In addition to checking your blood sugar, your doctor should check your serum insulin levels every time he takes blood to make sure that if you do have hypoglycemia, it is not being caused by an insulin-producing tumor.

If during the 5 hour glucose tolerance test your blood sugar drops below a certain level, you must have the above mentioned symptoms to be diagnosed as having hypoglycemia. In the twenty-four years I have been practicing psychiatry, I have only found three cases of hypoglycemia. Don't let your doctor pass your symptoms off as hypoglycemia unless he has done the above test and it has come out positive. Treatment for hypoglycemia is very different than treatment for panic disorder.

In the case of true panic disorder, once the offending gene kicks in, you generally can't get it to kick out. Brain chemistry flips out of balance. All the talk therapy in the world is not going to get the brain chemistry to flip back into balance. A therapist can no more talk a person out of panic attacks than he can talk a person out of a broken leg. It will require a combination of talk therapy and medication therapy to get the brain chemistry to flip back into balance and keep it there. If done properly, this returns your brain to normal functioning and does not dope you up or space you out.

> Jimmy began having panic attacks at the age of seventeen after he and several friends were crawling around in freshly buried sewer pipes. Every once in a while they would come to a place where they could see the surface and would poke their heads out. As they kept going, they came to several places where they could not get out. They were completely in the dark, and Jimmy became panicky. He turned and went into a "blind run" in order to get back to the opening. He knocked down and ran over the people who were behind him.
>
> He had been having panic attacks since that time when he got into situations where he felt

as though he was going to lose control and embarrass himself in public. This increased to the point that he was unable to travel beyond a 15 mile radius from his home. He got panicky in tunnels, elevators and other closed areas and was unable to tolerate them. He would drive thirty minutes out of his way to avoid going through a tunnel. This worsening condition had compromised his lifestyle, but he was able to get a job as a fireman. He was able to function in a limited way when he came in for treatment at the age of 36.

Soon after starting the medication, the panic attacks became controlled. He was able to desensitize quickly and was able to do whatever he wanted. His biggest thrill was being able to drive his kids to Disney World without problems after just seven months of treatment. He could have gone sooner, but he had to wait for his summer vacation.

The brain is the organ that controls emotion and behavior. Just as things can go wrong with the heart, liver, lungs, etc., things can also go wrong with the brain. If this happens to occur in the part of the brain that regulates or produces emotion or behavior then emotion or behavior can become sick (mental illness). Many mental illnesses such as panic disorder, obsessive compulsive disorder, depression, mania, schizophrenia, hyperactivity, dyslexia and others are caused by physical changes in the brain. These are real, not imagined, faked or exaggerated as many people and insurance companies believe. It is the job of the psychiatrist to figure out what is wrong with the brain and then figure out how to fix it.

The part of the brain that produces emotion is called the

limbic system (see diagram #1). It consists of the hippocampus, amegdala, mammilary bodies and hypothalamus. Hippocampus translated from Latin means sea horse. Supposedly to neuroanatomists it looked like a sea horse lying on its back. The hippocampus is responsible for mood and is necessary for memory. In its mouth is the amegdala or translated from Latin, almond. The amegdala is responsible for turning on anger, aggression and pleasure and is responsible for turning it off. At its tail are the mammilary bodies. The specific function of the mammilary bodies is unknown. All of these areas together produce emotion and are necessary for memory. The thalamus is centrally located deep within the brain, and all incoming sensory stimuli (sight, sound, smell, touch, taste and proprioception - awareness of the location of your body parts) arrive here. The hypothalamus is hypo (below) the thalamus and coordinates all incoming sensory stimuli between the thalamus, the cortex and the pituitary gland. The cortex is where consciousness is located in the brain. The pituitary gland is the master endocrine gland and regulates the thyroid, parathyroid, adrenal, genital and thymus glands. It is the connection between the brain and the endocrine system. The limbic system coordinates mood and emotion with the body and brain in addition to regulating the endocrine system and the immune system. The limbic system also produces primal behaviors and emotions of self-preservation.

When an alerting stimulus comes into the brain, it stimulates the locus ceruleus (blue spot) in the upper brain stem (see diagram #1). This excites the reticular activating system, a nerve pathway, which fires to the limbic system and to the cortex, and you become aware you are alert. It also fires down the spinal cord preparing your body for "fight or flight." There are supposed to be numerous checks and balances to regulate and fine tune the locus ceruleus. It should relax and turn off if there is no reason to be alert. However, in people with panic attacks, their locus ceruleus genetically doesn't have the ability to do this. If this pathway continues to fire, it leads you to experience all the symptoms of panic attacks, and your cortex learns and remembers where you were and what you were doing at the time. You then become sensitized to those experiences. The next time you have a similar experience the cortex helps stimulate the locus ceruleus. You become trapped in an ever expanding syndrome called panic disorder with phobias. As you can see, it feeds on itself in a vicious cycle.

Talk therapy can help break the cycle by helping you understand what is going on and gives you tools to control it. It **is** in your head, literally, and it is **not** imagined. It is very real!

Medication therapy also helps break the cycle by putting the brain chemistry back into balance. The brain is made up of billions of nerve cells called neurons. Each neuron is a carbon-based computer chip or integrated circuit. Our home computers use silicon-based chips. The three pound computer you carry in your head is many times more sophisticated than the most advanced computers built.

The neurons are electro-chemical organs (see diagram #2) that send and receive information to and from other neurons. Some of the information coming in is excitatory (excites the neuron into firing off electrically) and some is inhibitory (inhibiting the neuron from firing off electrically). This is where the balance comes in. The neuron integrates the information and fires off at a frequency or rate based on the summation of the information being received.

When it fires, an electrical charge flows down the outside of the neuron until it reaches the end (see diagram #3). There is a space between this neuron and the next. The space is called a synapse. A spark doesn't jump across the synapse. Instead a chemical is released. This chemical is called a neuro-transmitter.

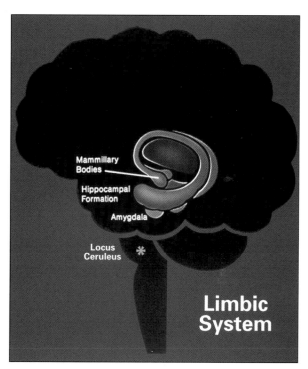

Diagram #1

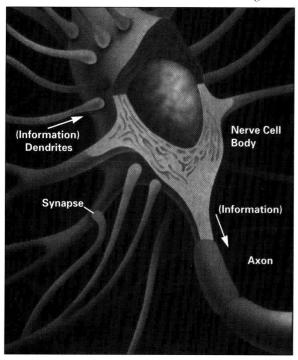

Diagram #2

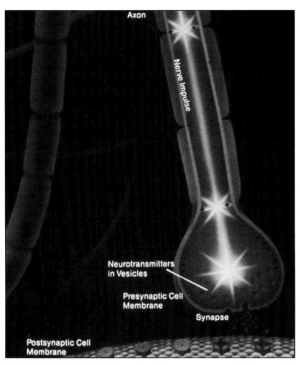

Diagram #3

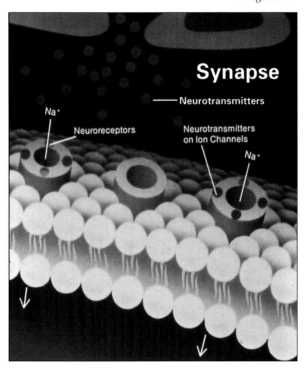

Diagram #4

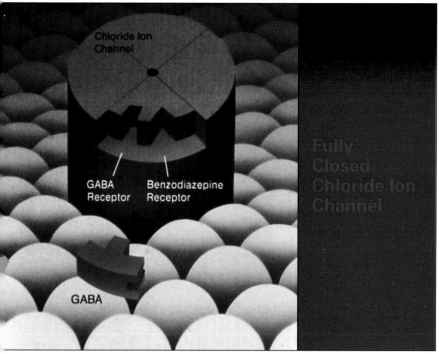

Diagram #5

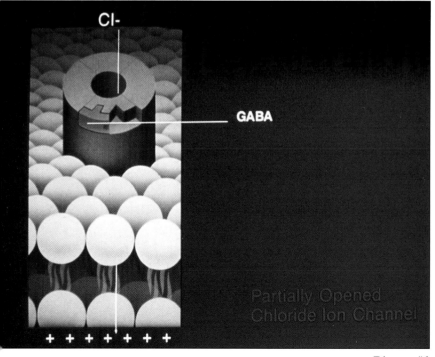

Diagram #6

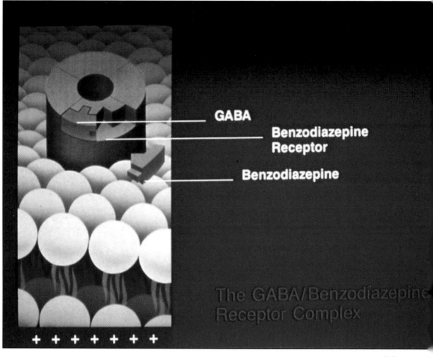

GABA

Benzodiazepine Receptor

Benzodiazepine

The GABA/Benzodiazepine Receptor Complex

+ + + + + + + +

Diagram

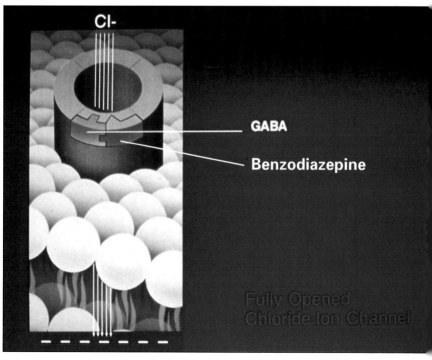

Cl-

GABA

Benzodiazepine

Fully Opened Chloride Ion Channel

– – – – – –

Diagram

There are over 200 known neurotransmitters, and we only understand what approximately 50 of them do. We are still near the stage of stone knives and bear skins in psychiatry. However, we understand enough to produce medications that alter the neurotransmitters and can use these medications effectively to change the amounts of neurotransmitters present and rebalance them back to normal.

Each neurotransmitter fits like a key into a lock on a receptor site on the receiving neuron (see diagram #4). When this happens, it causes a chemical reaction to take place. If enough of this chemical reaction occurs, it causes an electrical reaction and the message is transmitted.

This diagram shows an excitatory neurotransmitter, norepinephrine. When it fits into place on its receptor site, it opens the sodium ion channel and allows sodium ions with a positive charge (Na^+) to flow into the nerve cell. This causes a change in the electrical charge across the nerve cell membrane. When that electrical charge reaches a certain threshold, the nerve fires off electrically.

Stress, tensions, anxiety and physical illnesses such as a broken bone or a cold, as well as stimulating chemicals like caffeine and cocaine cause this neurotransmitter to be released.

The major inhibitory neurotransmitter of the brain is GABA-gamma amino butyric acid (see diagrams #5 and #6). This fits like a key into a receptor site on the chloride ion channel. When this happens, it partially opens the chloride ion channel which allows negatively charged chloride ions (Cl^-) to flow from outside to inside the nerve cell. This neutralizes the positively charged sodium ion (Na^+) 1 for 1 and cancels it out, decreasing the excitement.

If there are too many stresses, the brain has a backup system. The brain produces its own benzodiazepine tranquilizer (similar to Valium, Librium, Xanax, etc.). It fits like a key into two receptor sites, one on the chloride ion channel and one on

47

the GABA molecule (see diagrams #7 and #8). When it fits into place, it causes the chloride ion channel to open more, causing a greater amount of chloride (Cl^-) to flow through, further neutralizing the sodium (Na^+). One genetic defect prevents the brain from producing its own tranquilizer at a high enough rate. If the stress you are under, physical in combination with psychological, is greater than your brain's ability to cancel it out, you get anxiety. If it is severe enough, you get panic attacks. You could develop depression or other medical illnesses. It depends on the gene or genes you have inherited. There are probably a dozen or more genes that can cause different chemical defects and produce panic attacks.

Modern psychiatry has been able to produce artificial chemicals - benzodiazepine tranquilizers - that fit into these natural tranquilizer receptor sites and - antidepressants - which rebalance brain chemistry in other ways. These medications allow you to rebalance your brain chemistry when you don't have the proper genes to allow your brain to do it on its own.

Although a benzodiazepine tranquilizer is the first choice of medication in the treatment of panic disorder, other classes of medications can also be effective. Antidepressants are sometimes effective against panic disorder. However, they seem to be more effective when a patient also has depression and the depression is the primary illness producing a secondary panic disorder. Often the antidepressants and the benzodiazepine tranquilizers have to be prescribed in combination when a combination of disorders is present. There are many possible types of medications that can be combined to obtain more effectiveness than any medication used alone. This is where the psychopharmacologist psychiatrist really earns his fee. Non-psychiatric physicians often make feeble attempts at combining medications that generally don't help, may produce more side effects and can be dangerous. Psychopharmacologist psychiatrists are trained to prescribe such combinations safely and effectively.

The major side effect of benzodiazepine tranquilizers is sedation. This usually occurs at the beginning of treatment. However, the patient builds a tolerance to this side effect with time. It is best to start with a low dose of medication and increase the dosage slowly until the panic attacks cease. This should then be maintained during the acute stages of therapy (2-12 months). In order to be effective, the medication must be taken every day, 2-4 times per day. One of the most common causes of treatment failure is too little medication spaced too far apart.

As long as the stress remains constant, the dosage of medication should remain constant. This is called the maintenance level. If the stress level increases, the medication will have to be increased. When the stress returns to its normal level, the medication can be returned to its maintenance level. Talk therapy and deconditioning reduce stress over a period of time which allows the medication to be reduced to a lower maintenance level or discontinued altogether.

Living in a high-tech, high-stress, late twentieth-century, industrialized society produces stress in subtle ways. Change causes stress. Our society, culture and environment are changing faster than our ability to adapt to the changes. When patients tell me they want to get off their medications, I tell them to stop listening to the TV and radio and quit reading newspapers and magazines. I tell them to quit their job, sell their house and move to the south sea islands and live on coconuts and fish. I urge them to take me along with them. If they are not willing or able to drastically reduce the stress in their lives then taking the medications on a long term basis is the only other way to keep their brain chemistry balanced and their illness under control. So far I have not had any patients take me up on my extreme suggestion about the south sea islands, but I am always hoping.

When the levels of stress are reduced by helping the patient desensitize and helping him learn healthier ways to deal with society, family and job then he might feel sedated on his usual dosage of medication. At that time, the medication can be reduced slowly and can be leveled out at a lower dosage if anxiety symptoms return. This becomes the new maintenance level.

Most patients will experience breakthrough anxiety especially during the early phase of treatment. This can occur at anytime during the treatment process or even after being discharged from care. This may even escalate to a full blown panic attack. Patients shouldn't worry if this happens. It does not mean that treatment isn't working and that the illness has returned to its pre-treatment levels. It just means that current stress levels have increased beyond the brain's or medication's ability to balance them out. This requires an increase in the dosage of medication.

If a patient experiences acute breakthrough anxiety or experiences a panic attack when on his maintenance dose of benzodiazepine tranquilizers, he can put an extra ½ to 1 pill under his tongue. That way it gets absorbed in 5-10 minutes rather than the usual 30-60 minutes when swallowed. The medication tastes bitter, but my patients prefer that slight discomfort to a panic attack. The trick is to get the panic attacks under control with the medication. This gives the patient control over the illness and goes a long way toward helping return him to normality. During the early phase of treatment, patients often tell me that they start to feel the panic attack coming on, but it stops somewhere below the point of becoming full blown. The medication is doing its job, but the patient hasn't learned to fully trust the medication yet. With reassurance and continued therapy, the patient will learn to trust the treatment. This will gradually subside and eventually go away.

Some patients carry extra medication with them in order to

feel in control of the illness. A few of my patients no longer require taking any medication but continue to carry their medication as a support should they need it.

Another, more bothersome side effect of the benzodiazepine tranquilizers is short term memory loss. This is dose related and goes away with reduction of dose.

The major side effects of the tricyclic antidepressants are dry mouth, constipation, dizziness when standing up too quickly, profuse sweating on a hot day and blurred vision. The tricyclic antidepressants can be sedating or energizing and can cause sugar and chocolate craving and weight gain. This does not mean you should not take them, but they cause somewhat more uncomfortable side effects than the benzodiazepine tranquilizers. That is why they are not generally the first treatment of choice. They have to be titrated up slowly and usually take 7-10 days before they begin to work and can take up to 30-60 days to have full effect. The dosage of the tricyclic antidepressants can also be reduced as stress levels are reduced.

There are a number of newer antidepressants on the market (Prozac, Zoloft, Paxil, etc.). These have fewer side effects and are much more tolerable. This is why they are the most prescribed antidepressants today. But they are no more effective than the older types of antidepressants. They also take 7-10 days to begin to work and can take 30-60 days to have full effect. They can also cause chocolate and sugar craving and weight gain. Their most troubling side effects are decreased sex drive and insomnia.

The most effective medications for panic disorder are the monoamine oxidase inhibitor antidepressants (MAOI's): Nardil, Parnate and Marplan. Nardil is the most effective MAOI for panic disorder. The major side effects are insomnia, agitation and lowered blood pressure which can produce dizziness. If combined with the wrong foods or medications, MAOI's can raise blood pressure to high levels. Rarely, this could cause a stroke or death. However, staying away from the wrong foods or medications is easy and should not discourage anyone from taking these very effective medications. This potential side effect prevents MAOI's from becoming the medication of first choice for the treatment of panic disorder.

Adjunctive (additionally added) medications may need to be prescribed along with your primary medications. These are usually used in much lower doses then when used alone and help reduce certain symptoms that the primary medication is not taking care of fully.

As stated earlier, sometimes the antidepressant medications are combined with the benzodiazepine tranquilizers when depression is also present or to help reduce the anxiety.

The beta-blockers such as Inderol (Propranalol) is sometimes added to the primary medication. This is usually done when the symptoms of pounding, racing heart (palpitations), tremor and anxiety break through when a person has to perform, give a speech or interact in front of a large group. This medication will lower your heart rate and blood pressure and calm you so you will feel comfortable and, therefore, more self-assured. Sometimes physicians try to prescribe this alone as the primary medication, but it doesn't work very well alone.

When people have a great deal of trouble with sweating during the day or prior to interacting in a group, Catapres is often helpful. I have treated patients who literally have sweat dripping from their hands and pouring from their underarms. Adding Catapres to their primary medication often helps turn the faucet off. Using Dry Sol for the underarms can also be helpful. This is an over-the-counter product and can be purchased at your pharmacy.

People who are under extreme stress because of short-term, environmental pressures might need very small doses of a neuroleptic medication added to their primary medication. These medications such as Thorazine, Mellaril, Stelazine,

Haldol, Navane, etc. are primarily used as anti-psychotic (anti-crazy) medications in much higher doses for patients suffering from schizophrenia or mania. In very small doses, they reduce anxiety by a different nerve pathway than do the benzodiazepine tranquilizers or the antidepressants, so the combination hits the stress from two different directions. Caution must be observed here because there is a very small chance of getting a side effect called tardive dyskinesia. This causes twitching movements of certain muscle groups. If caught early and the medication is stopped, it goes away. If these medications are used short-term (1 week to 6 months), the risks of getting this side effect is extremely small. A psychiatrist should easily recognize this side effect if it occurs, and I would not be frightened to prescribe or take these medications.

BuSpar and Vistaril (Atarax) are both <u>non</u> benzodiazepine tranquilizers. They have minimal effect on panic attacks when used alone but can be helpful when added to and combined with the benzodiazepines.

As you can see there are many options for medications and combinations. A psychopharmacologist psychiatrist should be able to find the right medication or combination of medications for you.

When you take any of these medications properly, you should feel normal - not high, not drugged out - but normal! These medications are very safe and effective when prescribed and monitored correctly. This is a job only a psychiatrist is specially trained to do. Your family doctor is able to prescribe the medications, but he is not an expert at it and usually does not monitor them as closely as a psychiatrist. He should prescribe these medications in only the simplest of cases.

Likewise, a psychiatrist is able to prescribe medications for high blood pressure, diabetes, heart disease, etc., but he is not an expert at this and generally leaves it to those who are more skilled than he is. As "managed care" becomes the buzz word in health insurance for reducing cost and family doctors become the heroes of the day, be careful that the quality of your medical care is not compromised. Insist on seeing a psychiatrist and insist he see you for a long enough period of time that is comfortable for you. Managed care health insurance and HMO's often limit the therapy sessions to time periods that are too brief.

Remember that no one is capable of being an expert in all the medical fields. This is why we have medical specialists. Specialists are experts in their field. Don't let the government, your insurance company or your employer sell you a bill of goods. The quality of your medical care IS going to be compromised if your access to specialists is blocked. The combined training of a psychologist, social worker or counselor in conjunction with your family doctor does not equal the training of a psychiatrist. YOU must demand quality. It will reduce your suffering and your employer's medical insurance bill drastically. Insurance companies must realize that mental health is just as important as physical health. The two cannot be separated! Many studies show that adequate mental health insurance benefits significantly reduce the total cost of medical care, but for some reason the insurance industry and corporate America continue to turn a blind eye toward that fact.

Many people fear medications are a crutch and that taking them means they are psychologically weak and that they will become addicted to them.

The media has hyped this myth way out of proportion. It started with the 1960's book *Valley of the Dolls* about young Hollywood starlets becoming addicted to barbiturates and abusing alcohol. Both of these addictions are real problems and often happen. But barbiturates are not tranquilizers. They are a completely different chemical class of medications. Because of their addictive and abusive potential, barbiturates are rarely prescribed today.

The next book to reinforce this belief was *I'm Dancing As Fast As I Can* published in 1978. This book was supposedly about a "Valium induced breakdown." At that time, Valium was the most widely prescribed medication in the United States. The person who wrote this book appeared to have panic attacks and was doing fine while taking Valium until she decided to stop taking it because she feared she was addicted to it. She claimed her psychiatrist inappropriately advised her to discontinue it cold turkey. She then went through Valium withdrawal, and her boyfriend of 5 years beat her and kept her trapped in her apartment for weeks. When she did get help, it was described as poor quality help and caused her two psychiatric hospitalizations. She blamed all of her problems on Valium instead of on her boyfriend, on herself and on the perceived lousy psychiatric care that she had received. I suppose abusive boyfriends and poor judgment don't sell books, but frightening experiences produced by the most widely prescribed tranquilizer and lousy psychiatric care do.

In 1979, Ted Kennedy was on the Senate Committee of Labor and Human Resources. He was considering running for the Democratic nomination for president in the 1980 election. He came out with the statement about "a nightmare of dependence" for patients taking Valium and Librium. He got millions of dollars of free press and came across as the knight on a white charger battling the greedy medical profession and pharmaceutical industry. Benzodiazepine tranquilizers and doctors have yet to recover the lost ground.

The next critics were several vocal psychiatrists who were trying to capture the media spotlight and improve their earning potential by shouting that psychiatric medications kill people, burn out their brain cells, addict people and make them zombies. They also claimed that mental illness was just a myth created by the greedy psychiatric profession. It is amusing that they continue to treat mythical patients and practice their mythical profession. The media gave them the platform to make it appear that they were telling the truth to the public and that organized psychiatry and drug companies were evil and lying. They made it appear that medical fact was being kept from the public for the sake of profit.

According to the *Los Angeles Times* and many other exposés, L. Ron Hubbard, author of *Dyanetics - The Modern Science of Mental Health,* jumped on board. He founded the Church of Scientology. Although he died in 1986, the Church continues to flourish and for many years subtly pumped the media with inaccurate information - tranquilizers are highly addictive, Prozac makes you kill people if not yourself and Ritalin makes you violent. These statements are way off base and dangerous. Not only do they frighten people from starting medication, but they also cause people to abruptly discontinue their medications. This can be very dangerous and can even be life threatening. In addition, they cause people to become unnecessarily fearful of getting proper treatment. After all, what is bad for psychiatrists is good for the Church. The Church of Scientology is in direct competition with psychiatrists and all mental health professionals. Their masterfully planned campaign was designed to take patients away from psychiatrists and other mental health professionals through fear and bring them into their cult. The more followers they acquired, the more money and power they gained.

The media, as usual, jumped on this sensationalized band wagon, and instead of reporting responsibly, it reported stories blown far from reality for the sake of ratings. The media had a feeding frenzy with the inaccurate information provided by the Church of Scientology and hyped it to its limits. They have yet to spend as much time and effort correcting the misconceptions they helped to create. The media should be held accountable for the damage it has done to the mental health profession, to psychiatry, to the pharmaceutical companies and, most of all, to the patients they have frightened from getting effective care and to the patients who abruptly discontinued their medications and experienced withdrawal or return of their illness.

The American Psychiatric Association, Harvard University, the University of Michigan and the National Institute of Mental Health among others have put together comprehensive reports about the benzodiazepine tranquilizers (Valium, Librium, Xanax, Ativan, Serax, Tranxene). These reports included a review of the medical literature about these medications, and they read like a "Who's Who" in psychiatric research. All come to the same conclusions:

1) Benzodiazepine tranquilizers are safe and effective.

2) No tolerance develops to the antianxiety effects.

3) Tolerance does develop to the sedating side effects.

4) Withdrawal does not occur if withdrawn properly.

5) Some people (including those with panic attacks) will require the medications for their lifetime, and they are safe and effective to take.

6) 98% of people taking these medications take them appropriately.

7) Only 2% of people taking these medications abuse them in addition to abusing alcohol and street drugs at the same time.

The addictive potential of benzodiazepines has to be put into its proper perspective. People can become addicted to anything - TV, video games, injecting anything (including water) into their veins. One in 3 people will become addicted to heroin. One in 6 will become addicted to cocaine. One in 10 will become addicted to alcohol. One in 40,000 people **may** become addicted to benzodiazepines. Taking medications under the direction and supervision of a qualified physician is much safer than allowing your illness to go untreated.

If you have panic attacks and phobias, see a board certified psychiatrist. He is best qualified to diagnose the condition and treat it appropriately. He will first want to do an initial office evaluation. This should take about one hour. It may take less time in straight forward, uncomplicated cases or take longer in more complicated cases. He will instruct you to stop all caffeine and alcohol. In mild cases, he might want to try to reduce stress with talk therapy alone and allow the brain chemistry to rebalance on its own. In most cases, he will want to use a combination of medication therapy and talk therapy.

The therapy should include educating you about your condition. If you have read this book, you might know more than he does. If that is the case, switch to another psychiatrist. He should educate you about the different medications available to treat your condition and list the medication alternatives with his recommendations for what should be tried first. He should do a thorough medical history to rule out other medical conditions that can mimic panic attacks. He should order laboratory tests when necessary. As treatment progresses, he should help you learn to adjust the medications to your individual tolerance, circumstances and conditions. He should explore potential areas of stress including your childhood, family, marriage, job, finances, sexuality and social interaction. He should help you learn to better cope with and handle those areas of stress. Remember, he can only suggest change. You must put the change into effect. Finally, he should help you desensitize to any phobias that have occurred.

There are many ways to desensitize. It is more effective to

teach patients how to desensitize themselves. It is less costly for them; they do it in their own environment and at their own pace. However, the patient must be monitored for the progress being made or difficulties that occur. The patient should list all of his phobias from least frightening to most frightening.

After medications have brought the panic attacks under control, the patient should be instructed to put himself into his least frightening phobic situation. The anticipatory anxiety will likely build, but the patient should be instructed to stay there until the anxiety goes away. If it becomes unbearable or goes into a full blown panic attack, he should be told to put ½ to 1 benzodiazepine tranquilizer under his tongue and wait out the anxiety. Once it goes away, he should be told to return to the same place one hour later and do the same thing. This time the anxiety should not be as great and should go away sooner. He should return one hour later and do it a third time. By this time there should be little anxiety. He should be told to skip 1-2 days and then repeat the process. He should experience either no anxiety or reduced anxiety this time. Once he masters this phobic situation, he can go on to the next most frightening situation and repeat the same process until he has mastered all feared situations and circumstances. In some instances patients are afraid to take the first step. This is where a supportive family member or friend can help out by going with them as their "safe person." Occasionally, hypnosis might be necessary to get the patient over the first hurdle.

Each person is unique. Just as fingerprints, faces and bodies are unique so are brains, brain chemistry and personalities. People respond differently to each medication although the usual response is going to be similar. Some people will require very high doses of medications. Some will only be able to tolerate very small doses of medications. Some will require combinations of medications. Some will require intensive therapy. Some will require minimal therapy. The point is that each person's problems will be unique. It is the psychiatrist's job to figure all this out and provide the treatment plan that is most likely to help each patient and adjust it to meet that patient's needs. If certain techniques aren't working, it is inappropriate to continue them. The patient would be better served by changing that part of treatment or by changing the entire treatment to something that might be more effective.

David had several vague panic attacks in high school after using marijuana at age 18. He stopped using marijuana and had no further problems until the birth of his second child when he was 29 years old.

This child was born with major birth defects including defects of the heart. She died within six months of birth after undergoing several open-heart operations and numerous, costly medical procedures.

He began having full blown panic attacks on a daily basis and spent all his time thinking and worrying about them. The acute attack lasted ten minutes and then lingered for five to six hours. When he got a panic attack, he had chest pains, felt like he was going to have a heart attack and die. He had palpitations. He felt like he was going to go crazy and lose control of himself. He had numbness in his fingers and arms, and his arms ached. He experienced dizziness, sweating, diarrhea, decreased appetite and fear that he was going to vomit. He feared going to doctors, feared that he would be put into the hospital, feared having tubes put in his face, feared having surgery and dying.

After having a panic attack on a bridge, he became fearful of bridges. He could cross them but was very uncomfortable doing so. He didn't like dark places or crowded spaces and felt uncomfortable in them. He didn't like airplanes but would fly.

He went to a psychiatrist who diagnosed anxiety and prescribed a tranquilizer. He was too fearful of taking the medication, so he only took a few and then stopped the medication and refused further treatment until his wife became pregnant again.

The panic attacks and anxiety became so intolerable that he had no choice but to seek treatment again. This child was also a girl, and his wife's due date was the birth date of his daughter who died.

His diagnosis of panic attacks, brought on by the stress of watching his daughter suffer and die, was clear. I had his wife join him on the second session, and I explained his illness, cause and treatment to both of them. Although he was still reluctant to take medications, he was convinced medications were necessary for treatment. We were hoping nothing would go wrong with this pregnancy and birth.

The medications brought the panic attacks under control quickly. I had him desensitize by going back to the hospital where his sick daughter was born, was treated and died. He was able to do that without problems.

His next daughter was born healthy and without complication. We tried reducing his medication, but the panic attacks returned.

They were infrequent enough to allow him to take the medication when needed. He was able to desensitize the fear of driving over the high bridges. At first he needed to use the medication before driving over the bridges. He is now able to do this without needing any medication.

He tried stopping the medications again and has now been medication free for one year. He is prepared to use varying doses of medication for his lifetime if necessary.

You should see major improvements within two months. If this does not occur, discuss it with your psychiatrist. If you are not reassured and feel uncomfortable with his answers, switch to another psychiatrist. Be aware. Some very difficult cases can take a longer time, especially if the patient is fearful about taking medications and won't take them at high enough levels or if the patient is too frightened to desensitize. The average patient should expect to be in full remission by six months to one year. About ten percent of patients can come off their medications and require no further treatment by that time. The other ninety percent should expect to be on some dosage of medication, usually a smaller dosage than when first starting treatment, and should expect to continue monthly to quarterly therapy for their lifetime. This is their maintenance level. This usually consists of a brief med-check visit (5-10 minutes). If there is a reoccurrence of symptoms, longer, more frequent visits and higher dosages of medication will be needed. After the crisis is over, the medication therapy and talk therapy can revert back to a maintenance level.

Panic attacks and phobias is a chronic medical illness, the same as any other chronic medical illness such as diabetes, high blood pressure or arthritis and can be controlled with a combination of medication and regular doctor visits. Taking benzodiazepines for your lifetime is not different than taking medications for any chronic medical illness for your lifetime. Taking one to two injections of insulin per day does not make you addicted to insulin and does not make you an insulin junkie. Modern medicine has found chemicals - medications - that can alleviate the symptoms and suffering of your illness. Would you deny yourself or a loved one that relief because of ignorance, inappropriate fear or stigma?

The medications can be safely discontinued, but you can get rebound withdrawal symptoms if the benzodiazepines are discontinued too quickly. Rebound withdrawal is where your original symptoms return at a higher level of intensity than originally experienced. You could have convulsions and die if high doses of benzodiazepines are abruptly stopped. If they must be discontinued, slowly reducing the dosage prevents rebound withdrawal, seizures and death.

Many medications produce rebound withdrawal. Inderol, for instance, is used to treat high blood pressure. If it is stopped abruptly, you could experience rebound withdrawal, and your blood pressure could rebound to dangerously high levels. This could cause a stroke or death. If reduced gradually, no rebound withdrawal occurs. However, your blood pressure would return to the elevated level it was before you began taking Inderol.

Similarly, if the benzodiazepines are gradually reduced and anxiety or the symptoms of panic attacks return, it is not rebound withdrawal. Counselors, social workers, psychologists and your family doctor may think this is rebound withdrawal or drug withdrawal. It is simply your illness returning to the original level that it was before the medications were started. This gross misunderstanding of the illness and the medications help create and perpetuate the myths of the dangerousness of using the psychotropic medications. They are safe and effective when used in the hands of knowledgeable physicians - namely psychiatrists.

We can't cure the genetic defects causing panic attacks yet, but this is probably around the corner. One day we will be able to plug a patient into the laboratory and find out which genes are involved in his case. Pharmaceutical companies will develop medications that are more specific for each genetic cause and that will produce fewer side effects. Eventually, through genetic engineering and recombinant DNA, we will be able to repair the defective genes. The horizon is bright with hope for a complete cure.

Armed with the knowledge in this book you should be able to find the right treatment to help you on your way to a normal, full, productive life.

Chapter 5

Therapists And Their Training

In order to get effective help, you need to become aware of the kinds of therapists available and the treatment they are able to provide. Therapists are also collectively known as mental health care providers.

Psychiatrists are medical doctors and treat patients. No other mental health care providers are medical doctors. They can neither prescribe medications nor order laboratory tests. They treat clients.

The term client is a euphemism used by the non-medical mental health care providers to reduce the stigma of having a mental illness. If you are a client, you are not sick.

Similarly, psychiatrists deal with mental illness. All other mental health care providers deal with mental health. Again, they have come up with a euphemism to reduce the impact of going to them for help. It is good marketing but just isn't honest. They will attempt to treat almost any person a psychiatrist will treat.

You need to be aware of the limits of your therapist's training and know when he is going beyond his level of expertise. He may not recognize or admit his own limits or may not be willing to tell you what his limits are. If he tells you he is not qualified to treat you, he loses a patient/client. In these days of deregulation, competition for patients/clients is fierce. Because of economics, many practitioners would prefer to keep a patient/client they can't treat rather than lose that patient/client to another more qualified practitioner.

You need to be aware of the amount of training your therapist has had. You need to know if your therapist is licensed or not. If you are seeing a psychiatrist, you need to know if he is board certified or not.

There are a number of different kinds of mental health care providers. "Psychotherapist" is a broad term which applies to a wide range of providers. They have widely varying levels of training and experience and offer talk therapy to people with a range of problems from mild to severe. Providers with titles such as "therapist" or "counselor" do not need a college degree and do not need to be licensed to open an office and practice. Moreover, every priest, minister and rabbi is in a sense a pastoral counselor, but some of them have received specific training in providing psychological counseling and others have not. A pastoral counselor has more training than a pastor who counsels.

Be aware that some therapists are called "doctor." This does not always indicate a medical degree. Some non-medical doctors will lead you to believe they are medical doctors. "Doctor" could indicate a PhD. - doctor of philosophy, PsyD - doctor of psychology, EdD - doctor of education, ThD - doctor of theology, DM - doctor of ministry, etc.

Some therapists who have not achieved PhD, doctoral level education, will not correct you when you call them "doctor" or will lead you to believe they are PhD's.

Some therapists will confuse you by telling you they practice "behavioral medicine" which is another term for therapy. Some PhD's, EdD's, ThD's and DM's who are not licensed clinical psychologists will lead you to believe they are. Often therapists will want you to think they have more training than they actually have. Let the patient/client beware! It is your mind; make sure you know who you are trusting it to.

Because of the many types of therapists available, it is important to be aware of the levels of training and capabilities and limitations of the specific kinds of therapists. The following chart will help you begin to sort out the differences in mental health care providers.

The years of training and degrees required are approximate as this is regulated individually by each state and can vary.

DIFFERENCES IN MENTAL HEALTH CARE PROVIDERS

TITLE	YEARS OF EDUCATION*	DEGREE	CAN PRESCRIBE MEDICATION AND ORDER LAB TESTS	LICENSED	BOARD CERTIFIED	CAN INTERPRET PSYCHOLOGICAL TESTS
Psychiatrist	12 yrs.	MD	yes	yes	⅔	yes
Licensed Clinical Psychologist	8 yrs.	PhD PsyD	no	yes	NA	yes
School Psychologist	6 yrs.	Masters	no	yes	NA	yes
Psychologist	4 yrs.	Bachelor	no	no	NA	no
Licensed Clinical Social Worker	6 yrs.	Masters	no	yes	NA	no
Social Worker	4 yrs.	Bachelor	no	no	NA	no
Licensed Professional Counselor	5 yrs.	Bachelor	no	yes	NA	no
Psychiatric Nurse Practitioner	5 yrs.	Masters	no	yes	NA	no
Pastoral Counselor	4-5 yrs.	Clergy	no	yes	NA	no
Substance Abuse Counselor	0 yrs	none	no	no	NA	no
Therapist	0 yrs	none	no	no	NA	no
Counselor	0 yrs	none	no	no	NA	no

* Years of education indicate beyond high school

Psychoanalyst – usually a psychiatrist but can be a licensed clinical psychologist or licensed clinical social worker. Requires 1-2 extra years of analytical training after regular training. Must go through own analysis.

GUIDELINES TO GETTING THE MOST FOR YOUR TREATMENT DOLLARS

Whichever practitioner you eventually choose, there are some guidelines to remember.

1. Always ask questions about your therapist's background and training.

    •   How much experience does your therapist have in general? How many patients/clients has your therapist treated with your condition? What is his success rate? What is his training in the use of medications?

    •   If your therapist is a physician, did he or she graduate from an accredited American medical school or from a diploma mill in Mexico or the Caribbean?

    •   Is your psychiatrist a medical doctor, M.D. or an osteopathic doctor, D.O.?

    •   Is your psychiatrist Board Certified by the American Board of Psychiatry and Neurology?

    •   For therapists who are not psychiatrists, ask about their backgrounds as well. How much education do they have? Where are their degrees from? Are they licensed or certified? What is their experience and success in treating your condition? What if you need medication?

2. Ask questions about your treatment.

- "How long should it take before I feel better?"

- "What is my diagnosis, and what is your treatment plan?"

- "Do I need talk therapy only, medication therapy only or a combination of both?" "How did you come to that conclusion?"

- "Why am I taking this medication?"

- "Are there other alternatives?"

- "What are the side effects?"

- "How frequently do I need to come in and for how long?"

- "Do I need any laboratory tests?"

- "What are your fees?"

- "How much will insurance pay? What is my portion?"

- "Can I still be seen if I don't have insurance?"

3. Be aware that the treatment can involve either talk therapy, medication therapy or both.

4. There is nothing wrong with discussing fees. Some patients need only medication - low cost. Not all treatment is as costly as long term talk therapy.

5. The services of a non-psychiatric medical doctor (general practitioner, family practitioner or internist) plus a therapist provide a less comprehensive combination of training, background and experience than the services of a psychiatrist.

6. Shopping for the lowest fee or settling for the least costly therapist recommended by your insurance company or HMO as a "participating provider," "preferred provider" or "contracted provider" does not assure qualified or appropriate care. These terms just mean that your therapist has agreed to accept a reduced fee for his services. These therapists are often counselors, social workers or psychologists. You may pay less per visit but may be in therapy longer, suffer longer or even get worse. In the majority of cases, the most cost effective care is the highest quality care. You will feel better quicker, will require fewer, shorter visits and will get back to your full, productive earning potential quicker. In the long run, a board certified psychiatrist, most often, will provide the least expensive care you can find.

7. Because of the public's confusion about training and qualifications and about the stigma of seeing a psychiatrist, many counselors, social workers and psychologists charge as much as, and sometimes more than, psychiatrists. Make sure you are getting what you are paying for.

Chapter 6

Danger Signals

This chapter will alert you to what you should consider to be danger signals.

I'M YOUR ONE AND ONLY

If your therapist seems uncomfortable or defensive if you feel the need to get a second opinion, grab your coat and run.

LET'S GO TO THE HOSPITAL

Some psychiatric hospitals have a policy of referring more patients to those mental health care providers who admit more patients to their facility. The more patients they admit and the longer they stay, the more patients are referred to them. Some mental health care providers may be more directly involved. They may own an interest in or may be an employee of the psychiatric hospital or the alcohol or drug abuse center.

This is not meant to imply that the majority of mental health care providers have their eye solely on the dollar bill. That is hardly the case. But there are abuses, and you need to be aware of them.

CULT THERAPY

Watch out for any form of therapy that is marketed on talk shows and in magazines as if it were detergent: either NEW or IMPROVED. "If you only buy our product, you will be HEEEEEALD." Cults may be psychological in nature - primal scream, EST; they may be "religious" in nature - the Church of Scientology, television healing ministries; they may be physical in nature - iridology, herbal medicine.

If you're going to be roped in by anything, choose the

detergents; they are cheaper in the long run, and the only thing you risk is the scorn of your neighbors because your clothes aren't whiter and brighter. At least your life and your ability to make free decisions for yourself will still be yours, and you won't waste your hard earned dollars.

DUMP YOUR MEDS DOWN THE TOILET AND BE FREE

Watch out for the "throw away your medications" advocates.

- Medications are very safe and effective.

- Medications have side effects, but they do not burn out your brain cells, and there is little or no risk of becoming addicted to them. Alcohol and tobacco are far more dangerous than any of the psychiatric medications.

- Consider the effects of your illness if it is not treated with medications.

- Abruptly discontinuing any medication without proper medical supervision may be very dangerous and could even be life threatening.

YOU ARE YOUR OWN BEST FRIEND

You are responsible for your behavior and the consequences of it. Realize that something that is said or printed by a professional is not necessarily true, or it may be true for some but not for others. If you aren't living the life you want, you need to begin making choices that lead you in that direction. You need to educate yourself about your condition and find the right person to help you gain control of it.

GUESS WHAT I HAVE?

Be careful not to sign up for the "Disease of the Month Club." Certain conditions end up becoming the darling of the talk show circuit. As a result, they become quite "popular" and are often overdiagnosed (for example, anorexia nervosa, bulimia and co-dependency).

WHY AM I DOING THIS?

If you feel uncomfortable with your therapist, discuss it with him and see what he thinks, but rely on your own judgment. You just may not click. Sometimes you need to do some searching before you find the right marriage.

Don't do anything in therapy that you feel is inappropriate and that makes you feel uncomfortable. Sex with your therapist is wrong, and he should never let it happen. You may have sexual thoughts or fantasies about your therapist, and they should be discussed with him when you feel comfortable enough to do so. But sexual contact between you and your therapist is something that should not happen under any circumstances.

GET THEM IN – KEEP THEM IN

You should have treatment goals and should periodically check to make sure you are achieving those goals. Patients can become dependent on their therapist. Certain conditions are life long and require that dependency. Others may be self-limited, but some therapists foster a dependency in their patients to keep their schedule full. If you are not making progress, discuss it with your therapist and seek a second opinion.

Chapter 7

Glossary

This chapter is a glossary of technical words that may be confusing or misunderstood. This glossary will help you understand what your therapist is telling you.

ACETYLCHOLINE: An inhibitory neurotransmitter which helps regulate muscle movement.

ACUTE: An illness which has come on suddenly.

ADDICTION: The dependence on a chemical where a physical need develops. When the chemical is stopped, reduced or sometimes kept at the same level, withdrawal occurs. This is true of heroin and all opium derived drugs, cocaine and all of its derivatives, methamphetamines, barbiturates, alcohol, caffeine and nicotine.

ADJUSTMENT: An individual's adaptation to his environment from a behavior or an emotion that is less functional to one that is more functional.

ADRENALINE: One of the catacholamine neurotransmitters produced by the adrenal gland and by the sympathetic nervous system. It is not produced in the brain or spinal cord. It causes most of the physical symptoms produced by fear, panic and anxiety. It is also called epinephrine.

AFFECT: Used interchangeable with emotion. It is the expression or perception of feelings or mood.

ALCOHOLISM: A chronic, long term illness where repetitive drinking of alcohol at varying frequencies occurs. A person must have alcohol-created problems in two of the following six categories in order to be diagnosed as an alcoholic: job problems, police problems, medical problems, financial problems, family problems or friend problems.

ALLIED HEALTH PROFESSIONAL: A person with varying degrees of training. They may or may not be required to be licensed by the state. Sometimes they work under the supervision of a licensed health professional. Sometimes they work independently.

AMEGDALA: Translated from Latin this means almond. This part of the limbic system is responsible for turning on and off anger, aggression and pleasure.

AMERICAN BOARD OF PSYCHIATRY AND NEUROLOGY: Comprised of sixteen physicians from varying medical disciplines who produce and administer examinations to test the competency of psychiatrists, child psychiatrists and neurologists.

AMERICAN PSYCHIATRIC ASSOCIATION (APA): The national organization of psychiatrists for America.

AMINES: Organic chemical compounds which contain one or more ammonium ($-NH^2$) molecules. This chemical is especially important to biochemistry and neurochemistry.

AMINO ACIDS: Organic chemical compounds which contain one or more ammonium ($-NH^2$) groups. They comprise 20 different chemicals which are the building blocks of proteins and some neurotransmitters.

AMPHETAMINES: Stimulating chemicals that are often abused but can be safe when used medically to treat hyperactivity, attention deficit disorder, narcolepsy and depression.

ANTICIPATORY ANXIETY: Apprehension when getting into a situation similar to one where a panic attack has occurred in the past with the fear that another will occur.

ANXIETY: The emotion of apprehension, tension or uneasiness.

AUTONOMIC NERVOUS SYSTEM (ANS): A part of the nervous system that unconsciously controls basic life functions of the cardiovascular, digestive, reproductive and respiratory systems. It is divided into the sympathetic nervous system and the parasympathetic nervous system.

BARBITURATE: Sedating, addictive drugs that were the precursors of modern antianxiety agents and sleeping agents but are no longer used as antianxiety agents and rarely used as sleeping agents because of their addictive and abuse potential. The non-addictive ones are primarily used today to treat epilepsy.

BEHAVIOR THERAPY: A type of treatment that attempts to change the behavior of an individual by adjusting the environment and the individual's response to the environment.

BENZODIAZEPINE: Medications that are used primarily as antianxiety, anti-panic and sleeping agents and are commonly referred to as tranquilizers.

BIOFEEDBACK: The use of machines that quantify unconscious body functions that help a person become consciously able to control or influence those body functions.

BIOLOGICAL PSYCHIATRY: A branch of psychiatry that views the cause of certain disorders (anxiety, panic, depression, hyperactivity, schizophrenia, mania, etc.) as caused by physical imbalances in brain chemistry rather than abnormally learned psychological behavior. Medication therapy is used as the primary line of treatment with talk therapy as the secondary line of treatment.

BOARD CERTIFIED PSYCHIATRIST: A psychiatrist who has successfully completed an approved 4 year psychiatric residency training program after graduating from an approved 4 year medical school or osteopathic school. This makes him eligible to take the psychiatric "boards." At this point he is considered board eligible. He then has to pass the written examination before he is allowed to take the oral examination of the American Board of Psychiatry and Neurology. Once he passes the oral examination, he is board certified. This process takes at least 1 1/2 to 2 years to complete after residency.

BOARD ELIGIBLE PSYCHIATRIST: A psychiatrist who graduated from an accredited 4 year medical school or osteopathic school and then successfully completed 4 years of an approved psychiatric residency training program. He is eligible to take, but has not yet taken, the examination of the American Board of Psychiatry and Neurology.

BRAIN: The organ of emotion, behavior, thought, judgment, and insight.

CATACHOLAMINES: A group of chemicals whose precursors are the amino acids tyrosine or phenylalanine and are transformed into the neurotransmitters dopamine, norepinephrine and epinephrine.

CENTRAL NERVOUS SYSTEM (CNS): This consists of the brain and spinal cord.

CHOLINERGIC: The nerves which are part of the parasympathetic nervous system. They are activated by the neurotransmitter acetylocholine. This neurotransmitter is derived from lecithin.

CHRONIC: An illness that has been or will be present for a long time.

COGNITIVE: The intellectual, thinking or logical part of the mind as compared to the emotional part of the mind.

COGNITIVE THERAPY: A type of treatment that uses the individual's intellectual, thinking or logical abilities to change his ways of interacting with others or with the environment.

COMMUNITY MENTAL HEALTH CENTER (CMHC): A system of mental health care delivery put together by the federal government starting in 1963 to bring mental health services to each community. It is financed by public funds. The majority of treatment is usually provided by partially trained or poorly trained therapists, counselors or social workers because public funds are limited. Fees are charged on an ability to pay basis.

CONTINUING MEDICAL EDUCATION (CME): Courses taken after graduation from medical school or residency which provide an updating, refresher course for physicians on various medical subjects. The course usually lasts 1 hour but occasionally lasts 1 - 5 days.

CORTEX: The outer portion of the brain where consciousness is located.

DENDRITE: A branching part of a nerve cell that receives incoming stimulus from another nerve cell.

DEPERSONALIZATION: Strange or unreal feelings related to the self. For example, feeling that your mind is outside your body or that your arms or legs are detached from your body or belong to someone else.

DEREALIZATION: Feelings of unreality in relation to the environment. For example, feeling like things appear two dimensional rather than three dimensional. The appearance that time and movements are in slow motion. The perception that sounds or colors are changing intensity when it is clear that they are not. The perception that objects are becoming bigger or smaller when clearly they are not.

DESENSITIZATION: A therapy process by which an individual is made less sensitive to bothersome circumstances or internal feelings. This is done by gradually introducing the circumstance or internal feeling until the patient feels comfortable with it.

DETOXIFICATION: The medical treatment of withdrawing someone from addicting drugs such as alcohol, barbiturates, amphetamines, cocaine or heroin by use of medications and hospitalization to minimize the withdrawal symptoms.

DIAGNOSTIC AND STATISTICAL MANUAL OF MENTAL DISORDERS (DSM): A publication of the American Psychiatric Association which officially classifies mental disorders and describes them. This has gone through the *DSM I, II, III,* and *III-revised.* The *DSM IV* was published in Spring, 1994.

DOPAMINE: A neurotransmitter belonging to the catecholamine class of neurotransmitters. This is an excitatory neurotransmitter found in the brain which helps regulate muscle movements. It is responsible for certain forms of psychosis when elevated in certain areas of the brain.

DRUG: An illicit substance bought on the street and used for recreation by altering one's mood, consciousness or perception. These substances can produce dependency or addiction.

DRUG DEPENDENCE: The psychological craving for an abused drug to alter one's mood or state of consciousness. It is also the requirement of a medication to keep a chronic medical condition under control, for example, insulin for diabetes, Zantac for ulcers, broncho-dilators for asthma, tranquilizers for panic disorder and antidepressants for depression. Drug dependence and medication dependence are very different but are inappropriately used interchangeably by the public and media.

DRUG TOLERANCE: The increasing need for abused drugs - narcotics, barbiturates, alcohol or cocaine - in order to get the same physical or psychological effect which was previously obtained by a lower dosage. If the drug is not increased in dosage, withdrawal occurs. This does not happen with the benzodiazepine tranquilizers although the public continues to believe this misinformation to be true.

EMOTION: Used interchangeably with affect. The expression or perception of feelings or mood.

EMOTIONAL ILLNESS: Disturbances in emotion, behavior or thought which are produced by social, physical, chemical, genetic, biological or psychological problems. They produce symptoms which can be lumped into diagnostic categories and indicate emotional or behavioral problems. Also known as mental disorder or mental illness.

ENZYME: A chemical produced by RNA which is produced by DNA, the gene. These chemicals regulate the rate of every chemical reaction in the body.

EPINEPHRINE: One of the catacholamine neurotransmitters

produced by the adrenal gland and by the sympathetic nervous system. It is not produced in the brain or spinal cord. It causes most of the physical symptoms produced by fear, panic and anxiety. It is also called adrenaline.

FEAR: The emotional or physical reaction to danger.

GABA (GAMMA AMINO BUTYRIC ACID): The major inhibitory neurotransmitter of the brain.

GENES: Made up of DNA. These are the building blocks of heredity. They combine in long strands to form chromosomes.

GLUCOSE TOLERANCE TEST (GTT): A blood test used to check for diabetes and hypoglycemia. After fasting for 12 hours, a standard amount of glucose (sugar) is swallowed. Blood is drawn at varying intervals and analyzed for the amount of glucose in it.

HEALTH MAINTENANCE ORGANIZATION (HMO): A relatively recent form of health care delivery system which has been given special financial incentives by the government in an attempt to reduce health care costs. It is supposed to do this by relying on the "gate keeper" (general practitioner, internist, family practitioner or ob-gyn) who is given financial incentives to minimize laboratory tests, minimize referrals to specialists and minimize treatment.

HIPPOCAMPUS: Translated from Latin means sea horse. This part of the limbic system is necessary for emotion and memory.

HYPERVENTILATION: Shallow, rapid breathing often associated with anxiety. This reduces the carbon dioxide content of the blood which produces symptoms of light-headedness, dizziness, feelings of faintness, tingling of the extremities, palpitations of the heart and feelings of respiratory distress.

INTERN: A medical doctor who has graduated from an accredited four year medical school or osteopathic school and is attending a one year general medical training program.

INTERNATIONAL CLASSIFICATION OF DISEASES (ICD): The World Health Organization's list of disease categories. This classification is mainly used for research purposes.

LIMBIC SYSTEM: The part of the brain which produces and coordinates mood and emotions between the body and brain in addition to regulating the endocrine system and immune system. It also produces primal behaviors and emotions of self-preservation.

LOBOTOMY: A type of non-specific brain surgery used in the 1930's and the 1940's prior to the discovery of psychotropic medications. This surgery produced drastic changes in personality allowing previously violent or excessively psychotic patients to be made pliable and compliant. The technique was easy and consisted of sticking a probe above the eye into the brain and cutting off the frontal lobes of the brain. This was the only circumstance where a Nobel Prize was given and later rescinded. This technique is no longer used today and is considered barbaric.

LOCUS CERULEUS: Located in the upper part of the brain stem. It is responsible for receiving alerting stimuli and sending the alerting stimulus on to the limbic system and cortex of the brain and on to the body to prepare it for "fight or flight."

MAMMILARY BODIES: A part of the limbic system whose specific function is unknown.

MEDICATION: A chemical prescribed by a medical doctor to treat an illness.

MENTAL DISORDER: Disturbances in emotion, behavior or thought which are produced by social, physical, chemical, genetic, biological or psychological problems. They produce symptoms which can be lumped into diagnostic categories and indicate emotional or behavioral problems. Also know as emotional illness or mental illness.

MENTAL HEALTH: A relative term indicating a lack of major emotional, behavioral or thinking problems. Good mental health allows success at the job, allows intimacy and allows successful interpersonal, environmental and social interaction.

MENTAL ILLNESS: Disturbances in emotion, behavior or thought which are produced by social, physical, chemical, genetic, biological or psychological problems. They produce symptoms which can be lumped into diagnostic categories and indicate emotional or behavioral problems. Also known as emotional illness or mental disorder.

MITRAL VALVE: The heart valve between the chambers of the left side of the heart.

MONOAMINE OXIDASE (MAO): An enzyme located both inside and outside nerve cells which break down certain neurotransmitters making them unusable.

MONOAMINE OXIDASE INHIBITOR (MAOI): A category of antidepressant medications that block or inhibit the enzyme monoamine oxidase, not only in the brain but throughout the body which increases the levels of certain neurotransmitters. The therapeutic effect comes from the increase of neurotransmitters in the brain. The major side effect, elevated blood pressure when eating certain foods or combing certain medications, comes from the increase in neurotransmitters throughout the body.

MOOD: An all encompassing emotion that flavors one's experience of the world.

NARCOTIC: Any chemical derived from opium or that can be synthesized as opium-like. It often causes addiction by altering one's mood or state of consciousness. It is used in medicine to alleviate pain.

NERVOUS BREAKDOWN: A non-specific, non-medical term indicating some form of mental disorder.

NEURON: A nerve cell. The basic unit of the nervous system.

NEUROTRANSMITTER: A chemical produced by nerves that allows information to be transferred from one nerve to the next. Examples are: epinephrine (adrenaline), norepinephrine (noradrenalin), dopamine, seratonin, acetylcholine, GABA.

NOREPINEPHRINE: A neurotransmitter belonging to the catacholamine class of neurotransmitters which seem to have an effect on mood. If the levels are too high, elevated mood or mania occurs. If the levels are too low, unhappiness or depression occurs. Also called noradrenalin.

OPIATE: Any one of a number of chemicals produced from opium or produced synthetically to resemble opium. Opiates generally dull one's internal and external feelings. They can produce a sense of well being and can become addictive. They are used in medicine to relieve pain.

PALPITATIONS: A strong, rapid heart beat associated with the feeling that your heart is going to jump out of your chest.

PANIC: The sudden experience of overwhelming fear, terror, anxiety or impending doom.

PANIC ATTACK: A spontaneous, sudden, unexpected, brief episode of sheer terror when there is no reason to be fearful.

PANIC DISORDER: A mental illness where at least 4 panic attacks have occurred in a four week period or the attacks are followed by the fear of having another attack.

PARASYMPATHETIC NERVOUS SYSTEM: The other half of the autonomic nervous system which unconsciously regulates normal life functions such as heart rate, digestion and breathing during normal, non-dangerous conditions.

PASTORAL COUNSELOR: A member of the clergy given specific training in therapeutic techniques. They can set up practices on a fee for service basis but must be licensed to do so. Not all pastors who counsel have had special training in therapeutic techniques.

PHOBIA: A continuous, unrealistic, extreme fear of a specific situation or object and the avoidance of that situation or object no matter what.

PHOBIC AVOIDANCE BEHAVIOR: Avoiding places or situations whenever possible where a panic attack has occurred in the past.

PITUITARY GLAND: The master endocrine gland of the body that regulates the thyroid, parathyroid, adrenal, genital and thymus glands.

PROLAPSED MITRAL VALVE: A stretching of the heart valve between the heart chambers on the left side of the heart. Once thought to produce panic-like symptoms but now known to be a variation of normal.

PSYCHOANALYSIS: Developed by Sigmund Freud as a theory of psychological development and includes a specific technique of psychotherapy. This generally includes three to five, one hour sessions per week with the patient lying on a couch and the therapist sitting behind him. The analyst provides little interaction with the patient until a specific interpretation is felt appropriate which he then explains to the patient.

PSYCHOANALYST: Generally a psychiatrist, but may be a psychologist or social worker, who has been trained in psychoanalytic theory and uses the techniques of analysis. This individual usually has gone through his own analysis.

PSYCHOPHARMACOLOGY: A branch of psychiatry where the psychiatrist is an expert in the use of medications which rebalance brain chemistry.

PSYCHOTIC: The psychiatric term for crazy. When a person's thoughts, emotions, judgments or perceptions are grossly impaired. The person is unaware of these impairments and this produces strange behavior. This is usually associated with schizophrenia and mania.

PSYCHOTHERAPY: A broad term used to indicate many forms of interaction between a patient and therapist where a change in behavior, attitude or emotion from an impaired one to a more healthy one is the goal of treatment. Also referred to as therapy.

PSYCHOTROPIC: Medications which alter brain chemistry

by increasing or decreasing different neurotransmitters in the brain.

REBOUND WITHDRAWAL: The return of the original symptoms of an illness to a temporarily higher level of intensity when a prescribed medication is reduced too quickly.

RECEPTOR: A specific area of a nerve cell membrane which allows a neurotransmitter to attach to it, effecting a change in that cell membrane, and allows information to be transferred from one nerve to another.

RECOMBINANT DNA: A term used in genetic engineering where DNA is separated to take out an unwanted gene or to insert a new gene.

REINFORCEMENT: A therapeutic technique by which an individual increases his therapeutic gains by being rewarded for healthy interaction and by avoiding the pain of unhealthy interaction.

RESIDENT: A medical doctor or osteopathic doctor who has graduated from an accredited four year medical school or osteopathic school, has completed a one year internship and is now embarking on specialty training. Some internships are now incorporated into the residency training program.

RETICULAR ACTIVATING SYSTEM: A nerve pathway which originates in the locus ceruleus and transmits alerting signals to the limbic system, to the cortex of the brain and to the body, preparing it for "fight or flight."

SAFE PERSON: A person trusted by someone suffering from panic attacks to return him home no matter what or to make sure medical help is provided should he have a panic attack while outside his home.

SERATONIN: A neurotransmitter found in areas of the brain associated with mood, pleasure, sleep, inhibition of anger, reduction of aggression and reduction of the perception of pain.

SYMPATHETIC NERVOUS SYSTEM: The other half of the autonomic nervous system that unconsciously regulates heart rate, digestion, breathing and sweating and prepares a person to respond to dangerous or threatening environmental situations. This produces the "fight or flight" phenomena.

SYNAPSE: A space between nerves where neurotransmitters are released providing communication from one nerve to another.

SYSTEMATIC DESENSITIZATION: A behavior therapy technique where the patient is asked to list his anxiety provoking situations from least threatening to most threatening. The patient is then presented with these situations starting with the least threatening until anxiety is no longer experienced. The next most threatening experience is then tackled and so on until the most frightening experience is conquered.

THERAPY: A broad term used to indicate many forms of interaction between a patient and therapist where a change in behavior, attitude or emotion from an impaired one to a healthier one is the goal of treatment. Also referred to as psychotherapy.

TITRATE: The technique of slowly raising or lowering the dosage of medication to minimize side effects or to prevent rebound withdrawal.

TOLERANCE: Building an immunity to the desired mental or physical effects of a street drug. This term is also used to indicate building an immunity to the side effects of prescribed medications.

TRANQUILIZER: A generalized term for medications that decrease anxiety or agitation. They are divided into antianxiety and antipsychotic medications.

TRICYCLIC ANTIDEPRESSANT: A class of antidepressant medications whose basic chemical structure consists of three rings hooked together.

WITHDRAWAL: A set of symptoms which occur when addicting drugs such as heroin, cocaine, crack, barbiturates, alcohol, caffeine or nicotine are not increased in dosage to overcome the effects of the tolerance that builds while taking them or when they are abruptly discontinued. The withdrawal symptoms are different for each drug. This term is also inappropriately used to indicate the symptoms which occur when prescribed medications, such as blood pressure medications and tranquilizers, are abruptly discontinued.

Notes/Comments

WHERE AND WHY THE MEDICATIONS WORK

The following two diagrams show the nerve pathways of panic attacks. They are important to understand because they explain where the medications work and why certain medications work better than others.

Most panic attacks appear to start at the locus ceruleus which is the alerting center of the brain. When this fires off, it feeds impulses to the parahippocampal gyrus which feed impulses to the anterior temporal structures. Both of these areas are part of the cortex of the brain and make you aware you are alert and fearful. The anterior temporal structures feed impulses to part of the limbic system. The limbic system is where emotions originate. The areas of the limbic system involved in panic are the amygdala, which links experience in reality or from memory to emotion, and the hippocampus, which links emotion to experience. Both of these structures are intimately connected in a two-way feedback loop from and to the locus ceruleus. When the locus ceruleus fires, you become alert and prepared for fight or flight. The locus ceruleus feeds back to the parahippocampal gyrus in a feedback loop which continues to fire off producing a panic attack. The locus ceruleus also fires down the spinal cord in a sympathetic storm causing the symptoms of a panic attack.

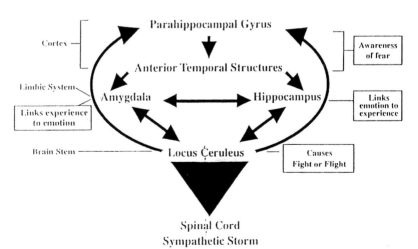

For anatomical locations of above see diagram #1 in book.

This diagram shows where the different medications effect the brain stopping the feedback loop which turns off or prevents the panic attack from occurring.

The antidepressants - SSRIs, Tricyclics and MAO Inhibitors - decrease the inappropriate excess stimulation from the cortex and limbic system decreasing stimulation to the locus ceruleus making it less likely to fire off inappropriately

The benzodiazepines work directly on the locus ceruleus quieting it down and preventing it from inappropriately firing off.

The Beta blockers work by blocking the physical symptoms of a panic attack from occurring at the spinal cord but do nothing about the mental experience of a panic attack. Without turning off the mental experience of a panic attack, the physical symptoms often break through. The Beta blockers are better used in combination with an antidepressant or benzodiazepine when necessary.

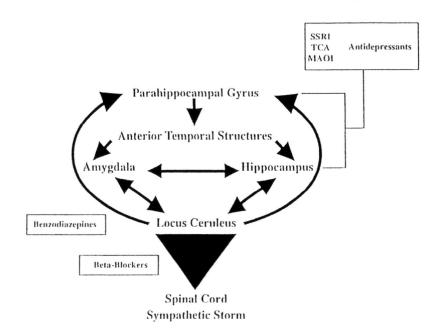

For anatomical locations of above see diagram #1 in book.

NEW INSIGHTS INTO WHAT TREATMENT IS BEST
Xanax, Paxil or cognitive therapy

The following discusses and clarifies the controversy of what treatment is best and most effective for panic and phobias: benzodiazepines, i.e., Xanax; SSRIs, i.e., Paxil; or cognitive therapy.

Since 1996 when Paxil was approved by the FDA for the treatment of panic disorder, it has become the treatment of choice for most physicians. Likewise, Xanax has been put on the back burner and many physicians will not even consider prescribing it because of its "addictive potential." How are you, as a lay person, suppose to understand the controversy and make informed decisions on what treatment is best, most effective and safest for you?

The benzodiazepines were first released in 1959 with Librium and 1960 with Valium. Ativan, Serax, Tranxene were released soon thereafter followed by Xanax in the early to mid 1980s. All the benzodiazepines work by fitting into the benzodiazepine receptor on the chloride ion channel in the locus ceruleus (See diagrams 1,5,7,8.). Xanax seems to make a slightly stronger connection. This receptor is there because the brain produces its own benzodiazepine. The anxiety disorders are stress related. When the brain can't produce enough of its own benzodiazepine to offset the stress, anxiety symptoms occur. The most effective way of relieving these symptoms is to add a synthetically produced benzodiazepine. The symptoms can also be relieved to some degree by various types of talk therapy, including cognitive therapy, to reduce actual or perceived stress. This is much more costly, time consuming and, for most people, is not as effective as medication.

The SSRI antidepressants Prozac, Paxil, Zoloft, Effexor and Luvox as well as the tricyclic antidepressants Tofranil (Imipramine), Norpramin (Desipramine), Elavil (Amitriptyline), Pamelor (Nortriptyline), Sinequan (Doxepin), Vivactil and the MAOI antidepressants Nardil and Parnate also effect the chloride ion channel and the benzodiaz-.epine receptor. However, they act on it in a secondary way, acting primarily on the seratonin re-uptake receptors in the limbic system

(See diagram 1.) which then effects the locus ceruleus in the upper brain stem. They all have an effect on decreasing anxiety, but it is much more subtle than the direct effect of the benzodiazepines.

Why are the SSRI medications getting so much positive press and hype? Why are all the benzodiazepines, especially Xanax the most prescribed, getting so much negative press? All the benzodiazepines are currently generic. The patent runs out on a medication after 17 years and then anyone can manufacture it as a generic brand. These medications then become inexpensive because many companies can manufacture them. They are no longer promoted to doctors or marketed to the public.

Since SSRIs are not yet generic (Prozac becomes generic 2002.), there is still lots of money to be made on them. Money pours into research institutions to test theories. Often the results are glowing.

Research institutions make millions of dollars each year by providing research to drug companies. Drug companies pay for the research on their drugs. Do you think a research institute would get funding for another project if their report was unfavorable to a sponsoring company's product? The FDA and Justice Department are currently investigating a multi-million dollar research fraud scandal. The researchers being investigated were primarily doing work on psychiatric medications.

Psychiatric illnesses are more difficult to do research on than other medical illnesses. Pneumonia or clogged coronary arteries can be seen and the amount of disease can be calibrated. Feelings, such as anxiety or depression, are much more subjective and can easily be over or under rated by the patient and research staff. This is not to say that all psychiatric research is bogus. There are good researchers out there doing honest research. One just has to be aware of the pitfalls here as well as in treatment.

Oftentimes drug reps who visit physicians or the media will present a single research paper showing a "unique" or "better" effect of their medication as compared to their competitors' medication. Many physicians as well as the media don't have the time to see if this claim is valid. Research theory becomes scientific fact when it is replicated three times by independent researchers. This is rarely done. My point is that there are many misrepresentations passing for scientific fact.

2

It is my opinion that the SSRI antidepressants are being over prescribed for panic disorder, and the benzodiazepines which are far more effective and much less expensive are being under prescribed.

The SSRIs work best when a person has a primary depression and secondary panic attacks or has primary obsessive compulsive disorder with secondary depression and panic attacks.

The SSRIs are safe, tolerable and effective but are not without side effects. They can produce insomnia in about 30%, nausea in about 20%, weight gain in about 10-15% of patients. There is a potential problem mixing them with other medications. They could cause blood levels of other medication to rise, sometimes, rarely, to lethal levels. The side effect of most concern is the reduction in sex drive in about 30% and to the point of no sex drive and inability to have orgasm in about 5% of patients. My point here is not to frighten you from taking these very useful medications but to let you know they are not the easy to take panacea the drug companies want you and your family physician to believe they are. They are very safe and effective when prescribed by a knowledgable psychiatrist.

SSRIs take 7-10 days to start to work and can take 30-60 days to have full effect. They can also make panic attacks worse in about 30% of patients, have no effect in about 30% of patients and work well in about 30% of patients. They work best if a patient has primary depression with secondary panic or has primary obsessive compulsive disorder with secondary depression and panic.

The benzodiazepines work directly on the GABA site in the locus ceruleus. If swallowed, they take 30-60 minutes to have full effect. If allowed to dissolve under the tongue, they take 5-10 minutes to have full effect. Xanax tastes very bitter but my patients prefer that to a panic attack. The other benzodiazepines have little or no taste. Benzodiazepines can cause sedation if the dose is too high. This can be counteracted by either lowering the dose or using small amounts of caffeine to bring down the sedation. They can sometimes cause memory loss if the dose is too high. Lowering the dose will get rid of that side effect. They can cause mild weight gain, 5-10 pounds, in about 15% of patients. They are abused by about 2% of the population who also abuse alcohol and street drugs at the same time. There is **NO** epidemic of misuse and this is blown far out of proportion to its reality.

One unique advantage of the benzodiazepines is to put one under your tongue for immediate relief if your medications are not holding your panic attacks in check. Their quick onset of action will allow you to remain where you are and finish what you are doing, rather than fleeing the situation and reinforcing your phobia. The benzodiazepines are safe and effective when prescribed by a knowledgeable psychiatrist.

Cognitive therapy claims to be effective in 90+% of patients with panic disorder. When you follow these patients long-term, you find that percentage decreasing with time. It is probably effective in about 10-15% of patients for over 2 years. There is a question in my mind if these 10-15% of patients would have achieved the same level of effect without any treatment. This has not been researched.

The biggest concern is for patients who don't respond to cognitive therapy or who relapse with panic attacks after going through treatment. Some might give up and not seek further treatment for fear that nothing will work and they are beyond help or feel embarrassed to return to their therapist because they were not strong enough to make this treatment work. Remember, this treatment does not require medication and the promised cure rarely happens. This treatment is strongly pushed by psychologists, social workers and counselors because they are not medical doctors and cannot prescribe medications. They do not want to lose their client to a psychiatrist who can both prescribe medications and do cognitive therapy. Oftentimes they will send their client to a non-psychiatric MD for medication. This physician is not as well trained as a psychiatrist to properly, effectively and safely prescribe psychotropic medications.

Having treated thousands of patients with panic attacks and phobias over the past 25 years, it is my opinion that the benzodiazepines (especially Xanax) combined with cognitive therapy is the treatment of choice for primary panic disorder. SSRIs and combinations of medications should be used when benzodiazepines alone don't provide full remission. SSRIs combined with cognitive therapy is the treatment of choice for primary depression or primary obsessive compulsive disorder with secondary panic disorder.

4